Finding Purpose In His Word

Linda J. Guy

authorHOUSE®

AuthorHouse™
1663 Liberty Drive
Bloomington, IN 47403
www.authorhouse.com
Phone: 1-800-839-8640

First published by AuthorHouse   02/24/2011

ISBN: 978-1-4567-5098-5 (e)
ISBN: 978-1-4567-5099-2 (sc)

Printed in the United States of America

Any people depicted in stock imagery provided by Thinkstock are models,
and such images are being used for illustrative purposes only.
Certain stock imagery © Thinkstock.

This book is printed on acid-free paper.

Contents

Acknowledgements   vii
Preface

Days   ix

1. Stay on the Wheel   1
2. You Are Justified   3
3. It's Time to Rebuild Your Temple   7
4. What Do You Have to Lose?   11
5. What Gear Are You Driving In?   15
6. Believe In Your Seed   21
7. Who Has the Power?   25
8. Can God Trust You?   27
9. Conquering Ungratefulness   31
10. Do You Want to be Seen?   33
11. What's Love Got To Do With It?   37
12. If You Are Not Growing…Check Your Fertilizer!   41
13. Bringing Things into Perspective   43
14. A Recipe for Success   45
15. Ask God for New Vision   47
16. Taking Full Responsibility   51
17. Wearing Jesus   55
18. What Do You Have To Fear?   57
19. A Sacrifice of Praise   61
20. Heed the Warning Signs   63
21. Run to Win   67
22. Seed that Falls on Good Ground   69
23. All He Wants is True Thanks   73
24. Don't Share It Until It Comes To Pass   77
25. Are You Getting Godly Council or Mere Opinion?   79
26. When All You Have Is Bread & Water   83
27. Strategy for Prosperity   87
28. Invite The Holy Spirit into Your Prayer Closet   89
29. Tough Love Is Better Than No Love   91
30. Let Your Testimony Be Your Witness   95

Bible References   97

Acknowledgements

My closest friend approached me one day and told me that the Lord had placed in her spirit to begin a daily devotional entitled, "A Word In Due Season" which would be sent to email subscribers on a daily basis during the work week. She also said He had put it upon her heart to add contributing writers to assist her with writing these devotionals, and after praying, my name came up.

Initially, I wanted to tell her…God gave this to you and not me… so you go forth in the power of His might! But somehow the Holy Spirit would not allow me to do that, and so upon accepting, I began writing with her in 2006. It was then I realized that what God was giving me to pen was actually ministering into the lives of others. So I thank my best friend, La'Kesha Ford Calhoun, for being obedient to the Holy Spirit's leading and pulling this book out of me, which is a product of the daily inspirational devotions. I love you girlfriend and sister!

I want to thank my parents, Robert & Willie Mae Peat, for raising me with morals, values and integrity. Thank you for training me up in the way that I should go…as you can see, although I strayed, I knew how to come back. I love you all so very much and thank God for having you as parents. To my Spiritual Father, Bishop Brandon B. Porter, who's supported me in whatever I sought to do; you know I love you. Thank you for your awesome teaching Sunday after Sunday, Tuesday after Tuesday…I needed every bit of it! To First Lady Melody G. Porter, you have been a joy to know and a pleasure to model. To the one and only Supervisor, Mother Ida M. Porter who has been a mother to me and a wonderful woman to know…I love you! To Missionary Patricia Meredith, you see I didn't have to wait on the mic…I've had an audience for over four (4) years (LOL). I love you!

To Pastor John Smith…thank you for allowing me to work with you in the adjutancy and for your spirit of excellence. I believe what I've learned under your ministry will take me far…it's greatly appreciated. Many thanks to those who prophesied my destiny to me...Prophet Todd Hall, Pastor Sam Moore, Apostle Lincoln and Prophetess Dent and Evangelist Ruby Holland Hutchins. I appreciate all of you being vessels used by God to affirm and confirm His plans for me. You all were in place when I really needed it the most.

Last, but certainly not least...to the best children in the whole wide world. We've have been through a lot...more than many know, but we have learned that God has not failed us nor has He forsaken us. He's always made a way for us when we needed Him and for that we are eternally grateful! I love you Brittney Danielle, Kaitlyn Ashley, and Victor Lowery Middlebrook. You all have made me a proud mother and I love you more than you can fathom. Keep your heads up and remain focused. God has great things in store for each of you and I can't wait to see His plans for you come to life before my very eyes!

Preface

Within the pages of *"Finding Purpose in His Word: A 30 Day Journey of Spiritual Inspiration"* are true stories and testimonials, which have been shared with thousands across the world. These testimonials and God inspired writings have touched the lives of many and have caused deliverance in the lives of its readers.

This book is the product of a daily email devotional, created for readers from the database of "A Word In Due Season Ministries," of which La'Kesha Ford Calhoun is the founder, and I have been a contributing writer since 2006. Wow! Look at God! If it had not been for my good friend, my Sister in Christ, my Blood Sister because we both have the same father; our daddy and Abba Father God…this book would not be in circulation! She pushed me when I didn't feel like writing; and when the Holy Spirit was inspiring me, she would call and say…"I'm not getting anything today, can you write?" Wow…how many times did that happen? Oh my!!

What you need to know most of all is that I share from the heart because God has challenged me to be transparent. Many times you will come across people who want to give you advice so that they can take the credit for helping you. What I have found in being obedient to the inspiration of the Holy Ghost is that when He gives me a word that blesses His people…I take no credit for it because I had nothing to do with. Why would I take credit for what only God can do? Who am I…but a vessel used by God. I love Him too much and know that I am only here because of His Grace and Mercy. Without it…literally I would be six feet under…and that alone is a testimony! God Bless You!

Stay on the Wheel

"Before I formed thee in the belly, I knew thee; and before thou camest forth out of the womb I sanctified thee; and I ordained thee a prophet unto the nations." – Jeremiah 1:5, (Background Jeremiah 18:1-6)

The story of Jeremiah's calling is a powerful example of how God chooses certain individuals who possess the character He is looking for, to do a particular job. Jeremiah had a bold calling on his life. It was to call a nation to repentance. And just like God chose Jeremiah, He has chosen some of us to do powerful things on this earth for the Kingdom. Our problem is that we don't realize the character we possess or we won't stay on the wheel (in His Will) long enough for that character to be developed.

In our background scripture, God woke Jeremiah out of his sleep and told him to go down to the Potter's house and when he got there he had something for him to see (and I'm paraphrasing here). Jeremiah didn't question what God told him to do, unlike us. When God tells us to pray for our enemy, that is what He expects us to do, because that may be the open door to our deliverance. Many of us will question God about simple tasks such as that...God, why do I have to pray for my enemy, they don't like me anyway...why God why?

There are three things we need to understand from this text:

$\left(\textbf{1}\right)$ **The purpose of the Potter** - The Potter decides the clay's purpose before it goes onto the wheel and He also decides what "qualities or character" this piece of clay needs in order to serve its intended "purpose." If you've ever seen a potter work with a piece of clay, then you know that in order for the clay to take its intended form, the potter never takes his hands off of the clay while "it is on the wheel." We must understand that God is the Potter and we are the clay. God has ordained a purpose for each of our lives, but character has to be developed within us to complete the purpose for which we were

1

designed. Never forget that God will be with you through that character building time, just as the potter keeps his hands on the clay during the molding process.

(2) **The purpose of the clay** - Because the potter has already determined "what" the piece of clay will be when it is put on the wheel, it is the clay's purpose to "yield" to the direction of the potter's hands. Jeremiah 18:4 tells us that the vessel was marred while in the hand of the potter, so he made it again. The word "mar" means damaged, hurt, disrupted. Yes, there will be times in our lives when we will endure hardship, heartache, and pain while in the hands of the Potter, but Hebrews 13:5b says *"He will never leave us nor forsake us."* If we go through the process, we will come out just as God has planned. I know it is hard to yield to the trials and tribulations in your life, but learn to accept what God allows. Yielding while in the Potter's hands is the safest place in the whole wide world to be...in His Will; because He has the power to make you whole again. I can't say it any better than Romans 8:28 *"And we know that **all things work together** for good to them that love God, to them who are the called according to his purpose."*

(3) **The purpose of the wheel** - The wheel controls the speed at which the potter turns the clay and has to be controlled by the Potter. The potter doesn't stop the wheel until it is time to take the vessel off. This is why it is so important for us to "Stay on the Wheel," because as long as we are on the wheel, we remain in His Will. If we stay on the wheel, God has the power to mold and make us the way He desires us to be. It is on the wheel where He can strip us of all impurities and make us clean vessels again. Jeremiah 29:11 says it best, *"For I know the thoughts that I think toward you, saith the LORD, thoughts of peace, and not of evil, to give you an expected end."* God has an expected end for each of us, but it is important for us to remain on the wheel to see that end come to fruition.

If you are reading this, and you happen to be dealing with something right now. Don't try to rush the process. Turn your will over to God and remember that no matter what test... trials... tribulations...disappointments or misunderstandings come your way, just be sure to "Stay on the Wheel."

You Are Justified

"For whom He foreknew, He also predestined to be conformed to the image of His Son, that He might be the firstborn among many brethren. Moreover whom He predestined, these He also called; whom He called, these He also justified; and whom He justified, these He also glorified. What then shall we say to these things? If God is for us, who can be against us?"

— Romans 8:29-31

Have you been more concerned with people's opinion of you than worrying about what God thinks of you? I have been guilty of this on many occasions. One in particular comes to mind.

I moved to a new city some years ago and I was struggling financially...just plain tore up from the floor up... BUT GOD! He seemed to make things stretch for me in those times when I should have lost my mind; but there was a prophetic word over my life that I would be stripped completely of all the old things in my life. I wasn't a good steward over my money, so there were many times that I had to move from place to place in order to keep a roof over me and my children's heads. During this time, God saw fit to allow my ex-husband to make the move to the same city right at the appointed time when I would be evicted for being habitually late on my rent. We were evicted and had no place to go; but God had already made the provision. I couldn't see it at the time, because I was caught up in what others might think of me and whether it appeared that I was living in sin again. I sat down with wise council and explained the situation and was given the green light. Proverbs 24:6 "Strategic planning is the key to warfare; to win, you need a lot of good counsel." The Message Bible

There was a humbling moment in this for me, because although these were his kids, I was no longer his wife and he was not obligated to do anything for me. So I did just that; I humbled myself and asked if the kids and I could stay with him in his one-bedroom apartment until I got back on my feet. He agreed to move our furniture into his apartment, so they were able to sleep in their own beds while there.

3

I took a spot on the floor in the living room. I went into a depression, because I was too busy worried about appearances and wanting to make sure that people knew I was living a saved and sanctified life...free of sin, regardless of the fact that I was living under his roof.

To allow me some space, my ex-husband would take the kids out of town on the weekends. As I was walking through the apartment some time later, the Holy Spirit spoke to me in the small still voice and told me that I was not justified by man but that it was He who justifies me. He said don't be concerned with what man thinks, and then Jeremiah 29:11 began to ring in my spirit; *"For I know the thoughts that I think toward you; thoughts of peace and not evil, to give you an expected end."* KJV

Read what the message bible says for Romans 8:33-39,

> *"So, what do you think? With God on our side like this, how can we lose? If God didn't hesitate to put everything on the line for us, embracing our condition and exposing himself to the worst by sending his own Son, is there anything else he wouldn't gladly and freely do for us? And who would dare tangle with God by messing with one of God's chosen? Who would dare even to point a finger? The One who died for us—who was raised to life for us!—is in the presence of God at this very moment sticking up for us. Do you think anyone is going to be able to drive a wedge between us and Christ's love for us? There is no way! Not trouble, not hard times, not hatred, not hunger, not homelessness, not bullying threats, not backstabbing, not even the worst sins listed in the scripture. They kill us in cold blood because they hate you. We're sitting ducks; they pick us off one by one. None of this fazes us because Jesus loves us. I'm absolutely convinced that nothing— nothing living or dead, angelic or demonic, today or tomorrow, high or low, thinkable or unthinkable—absolutely nothing can get between us and God's love because of the way that Jesus our Master has embraced us."*

What I'm saying to you is this, as a chosen vessel...as one of God's elect... your concerns should not be focused on what people think of you, but on what God thinks of you. As a son or daughter of the King, you can have what you ask, as you live in obedience to the almighty Father. When God justifies you, there is nothing man can say or do to change that; and no matter what people think of you, it cannot compare to what God thinks of you. Live in the abundance of joy knowing that God loves you and His love is unconditional.

It's Time to Rebuild Your Temple

"Is it time for you, O ye, to dwell in your ceiled houses, and this house lie in waste? Now therefore thus saith the Lord of hosts, consider your ways." - **Haggai 1:4-5, KJV**

Initially when the Lord spoke this to me, I was a bit hesitant in writing it. It was my week to write the daily devotional for an online daily word email distribution a very close friend of mine began. Because I was faced with so many obstacles in trying to get it out of my head and onto paper; I tried to write something else...but the Lord didn't see fit for the other writing to be shared. Although I am hesitant to be transparent...it is what God desires from those of us with a call on our lives. When we do things His way, He gets the Glory and we get the victory...so nevertheless, I had to be obedient.

When we take a look at the 1st Chapter of Haggai, we see a selfish nation...a nation of people who didn't care anymore about God's Temple...the place where His Glory resides. They got caught up in themselves and God had to put the mirror before them. Although this particular passage talks about the prophet Haggai delivering a word to governor of Judah, Zerubbabel son of Shealtiel, and to the high priest, Joshua son of Jehozadak: concerning rebuilding the Temple, it is a very compelling passage for those of us who's personal temples are laying in waste. I Corinthians 6:19 says, *"What, know ye not that your body is the "Temple" of the Holy Ghost which is in you which ye have of God and ye are not your own?"*

The people were really going through some difficult times, they had inadequate harvest and they were hungry, thirsty, and cold. Why? God was dissatisfied with them for neglecting to restore His house; and so He is with us when we neglect our Temples, which belong to Him. We wonder sometimes why we are suffering in our bodies or why we are experiencing some of the things that we are experiencing; but have you thought about your "temple" lately?

Isn't it odd how we can defeat the enemy in one area of our life...but then he seems to rear his ugly head in another area? It's because we have leaking roofs, broken door hinges, shutters hanging by a nail, paint chipping, rusty pipes...temple just plain ole' dilapidated.

There was an area of my life where the enemy would attack and I would get so angry and tired of that old slew-footed devil...but then God saw fit to bring me to a place of deliverance, and I said the enemy couldn't get me in that place again. All of a sudden I got comfortable, enjoying life, "in *my ceiled house.*" My prayer life began to change, my fasting habits diminished from 5 days a week to 2 days, down to... I couldn't remember the last time I was able to fast for 4 hours. My 5:00 a.m. meditation with the Lord changed to hitting the snooze on the alarm and taking just 5 more minutes, then 5 more, then 5 more, and then oops...I'm was starting to be late for work. You get the picture??? My temple began to lie in ruins and although the enemy could not attack me in that area of deliverance, he came at me another way...through one of my children. Oh, I forgot to mention that the nightly prayer with the children existed no more...not to mention slipping into their rooms at night anointing them with blessed oil...pleading the blood of Jesus over their lives... asking God to cover them and keep them from all evil. My Lord! Why didn't I see that my door was standing wide open...inviting the enemy in. Forget about the leaking roof, the broken hinges...I opened the door and welcomed that ole' hideous creature in! I was neglecting my temples; the one my spirit is housed in and the one my children lived in - and God was not happy with me.

God is not pleased when we, His children, neglect our temples! We have to make a conscious decision that nothing...and I mean nothing separates us from the love of God. Although our neglect may not be intentional, we must become cognizant that God is first and foremost. Yes, we talk to God on a daily basis...but God requires relationship and relationship takes work.

As the people began to hear the voice of the Lord, and then showing it by rebuilding the temple, He sent word through Haggai that He was with them. He allowed the faithful ones to see the results...or the fruit of their labor.

I don't know about you, but I have some rebuilding to do and the enemy has just been served his eviction notice!! Let's not forget God in all that we do...without Him we are nothing anyway.

What Do You Have to Lose?

"And there were four leprous men at the entering in of the gate: and they said one to another, Why sit we here until we die?"
— II Kings 7:3, KJV

I was brought up in the notorious projects of Cabrini-Green in Chicago, Illinois, where fighting was a common occurrence; and you had better show that you weren't afraid to defend yourself or you would get beat down! There was a mixture of residents such as Blacks, Italians, Latinos, etc., who lived in the high-rise. Some held down full-time jobs, while others were on welfare. Then there were those who were tied to drugs or prostitution. The children of the employed were somewhat alienated and even picked on if they looked like they had more than others. As a young girl…about 6 years of age or so, I can remember being dared to commit a certain act to prove that I wasn't afraid of the person who wanted to fight me. It went something like this: "I dare you to knock this stick off of my shoulder, or I dare you to cross this line" (line drawn in the dirt with the end of their shoe or with a rock on the pavement… (You get my drift?) Taking the dare meant that no matter what you do to me…you are not going to strip me of my dignity. Taking the dare also meant that you were calling the other person's bluff…to see if they were as big and bad as they pretended.

This type of environment was becoming detrimental to the very existence of each child growing up in that neighborhood. We watched as people took their own lives by jumping out of their apartment window, children being jumped to join gangs, and the homes of working families being robbed by those who didn't work. Ours was one in particular. So, what did my parents have to lose by getting out of this environment? What did they have to lose if they chose to leave? If they remained in the city, they may have lost one of their eight children to prostitution, gang banging, drugs, or eventually death.

One day my dad made a choice; he decided to pack up and leave;

not just the projects of Cabrini-Green, but the city as well. After all, what did he have to lose? If he chose to stay, his children may die or succumb to the affects of their surroundings, but if he left, we would have a better chance of surviving. So my dad quit his jobs (both of them) and moved back home to Tennessee. He was able to find work, build a home for his family, and then he came back to Chicago to get us. We left the windy city, never to return. Because of my father's brave decision that day, every one of his children is alive, working and raising a family. Everyone graduated from high school and some have college degrees. It was my father's desire that none of us would perish to the streets, so he made a conscious decision to get out while the getting was good. He made a decision to take his chances, besides, what did he have to lose?

In this story of the four leprous men, we have four men in a desperate situation…their backs were against the wall. These men had a disease that rendered them unfit for normal association… meaning, according to the law at that time, they were not allowed to live inside the city, but were to depend on charity outside the gate. Due to the disease, they were alienated. Because they were enduring a famine that had been prophesied by the Prophet Elisha, the lepers were desperate for food and water, but the gates to the city were guarded by the Syrian army. Now the lepers are sitting outside of the gate talking back and forth about what they are going to do…I could just hear them saying to each other…are we going to take this dare or are we going to starve to death…read what they actually said in verse 4: *"If we say, We will enter into the city, then the famine is in the city, and we shall die there: and if we sit still here, we die also. Now therefore come, and let us fall unto the host of the Syrians: if they save us alive, we shall live; and if they kill us, we shall die.* What do we have to lose?"

I will summarize chapter 7 for you. The lepers decided to call the Syrian guards bluff, who were supposed to be guarding the gate to the city. When they stepped into the camp, they discovered that it was empty…there were no guards, but plenty of blessings! What they didn't know was that God had already prepared the way for them to bring His word, spoken through the Prophet Elisha, to pass. What I'm trying to say is, sometimes we focus on our present situation or circumstance, not realizing that God has it all under control. When we look at our situations or circumstances with our natural eyes, we allow fear to set in and ultimately keep us from obtaining the blessings that God has prepared for us. Instead of becoming preoccupied with our problems, we should be looking for opportunities. I've heard my Pastor say on many occasions that "our extremities are God's opportunities," meaning: it is not until we have reached our limit that God steps in and finishes the process.

Hebrews 11:1 says, "Now faith is the **substance** of things **hoped** for, and the **evidence** of things **not seen**." I highlighted some words for the purpose of pointing out the leper's faith. They did not know whether they would find food and water on the other side of that gate, but they did know that they could die at the hands of the guards because they were forbidden to come inside of the gate. They **hoped** for food and water, but they found horses, donkeys, food, water, silver, gold, and clothing (raiment). What they found was not just enough for them, but more than enough to share with others. Because they stepped out in faith, God used them to bless others.

Do you desire a better job? What do you have to lose…trust God, then go and fill out the application or Bid Form. Thinking about getting that new vehicle you've always wanted? What do you have to lose…trust God, then go to that dealership and tell the salesman what you want. In need of a bigger home…stop contemplating, and go on the search for the house of your dreams. God is still in the blessing business…He has not changed. Don't allow fear to rob you of all that God has for you. Pray the Father's Will for your life…then ask Him to lead and guide your every step. The steps of a good man or woman are ordered by the Lord.

What Gear Are You Driving In?

"Ye did run well, who did hinder you that ye should not obey the truth?" – Galatians 5:7, KJV

This is quite a simple scripture...a question that needs no interpretation, but requires one to ponder in their mind on where you were in your walk with Christ when you first got saved to where you are now. Let that question marinate on your mind for a moment as I share with you my answer that God revealed to me.

In 1999, I went through a separation after a decade of marriage. I had gone through so much until I thought I would lose my mind. The separation was hard, because I knew divorce was imminent. During this period in my life, I not only separated from my husband, but I separated from my relationship with God...I was saved, sanctified, filled with the Holy Ghost and fire baptized prior to this stage in my life. I struggled with going forward with the separation and divorce because I knew that God hated divorce. But my circumstances caused me to "miss the mark" and therefore I was now in a backslidden state. I divorced in 2000, and shortly thereafter, made my way to a new city. While in my backslidden state, I went back to some of my old ways such as: going to the club, drinking, shacking with my boyfriend (because he told me we would get married...as if that made it okay)...all of these things were totally outside of God's Will for my life.

Then one day conviction began to set in and it was as if I could hear the voice of the Lord speaking to me when I was in quiet places. I woke up one morning and the Lord placed the church that I spent the last decade in upon my heart. I got up one Sunday morning and asked the Lord to help me get there, and sure enough, the Holy Spirit directed me to the church. I went, I heard the Pastor bring the sermon and then I left. After going back several times, I gave my life back to the Lord, (Hallelujah) but I still had a mess at home to clean up...I was shacking! Well, one day while on my lunch break, I decided to turn out the light and take a nap. While taking that nap...I began to hear the Holy Spirit comparing the stages of rebirth to the gears of a standard shift vehicle. I know this sounds strange, but even now God speaks to us in parables, or He uses allegories to help us understand what He is saying to us. As the Lord began to speak to me in that dark room, I jumped up and grabbed a pen and paper because I didn't want to miss what He was saying. I will try to bring this home so that you can see what I mean and what He revealed to me.

When He spoke about the 1st Gear, He revealed how it represented Newness-Rebirth. Second Corinthians 5:17 reads, *"Therefore, if any man be in Christ, he is a new creature: old things are passed away; behold, all things are become new."* If you've ever driven a standard shift car, taking off has its challenges. You have to keep one foot on the brake, while depressing the gas to begin your take-off. At this point you can hear the motor revving...anxiety, anxiousness, excitement increases because you are about to take-off. Have you ever noticed how anxious a person is when they first get saved? They are at church every time the doors are open...ready for the pastor to give them a word. They attend bible study faithfully...yearning for more of God's Word...running out to tell as many people as they can that they have been set free, and what God has done for them He can do for others...ready to witness. Romans 10:2 reads, *"For I bear them record that they have a zeal of God, but not according to knowledge."* Now they realize that there is not much time left to stay in 1st gear because the RPMs have maxed out and the car is beginning to jerk; it's time to change to 2nd gear. Understand this, the jerking represents something...it represents that struggle you are trying to let go of so that you can live free from sin... it's that shackle that you went to the altar to ask God to loosen and set you free from...it might be that old habit you want to break... lying, cursing, backbiting, gossiping, fornicating, adultery...you know what you are dealing with...just put your struggle in there. Mine was fornication. You see, the enemy only wants to keep us distracted...to keep us from going forward to the next gear or level in our lives; but we have to be determined to let nothing separate us from the love of God. Because of that determination, I found the strength to move out and get my own place...praise the Lord, Glory Hallelujah...I was on my way... I had Deliverance Street on my mind!

As we shift into 2nd Gear, we realize that there is just a little more time to linger here and you are able to give it just a little more gas. But take note, the motor is still revving…there goes that old enemy again, tugging at you trying to hold you back. Paul said it like this, *"I find then a law, that, when I would do good, evil is present with me"* (Romans 7:21). When you have become born again in Christ, the enemy tries to do everything he can to keep his clutches in you and make you feel like you are not going to make it without him. He wants to make you feel inadequate, unloved, used and abused. He may even call you in that sweet tone of voice…do you need any money…do you need gas in your car…can I take you to dinner…do you want me to pay your phone bill…what about the utilities…have you been shopping lately? He may take that old habit such as smoking or drinking and tell you that as long as you do it in the privacy of your own home…no one will know about it…but the enemy is stupid…because the eyes of God are in every place, beholding the good and the evil. Ephesians 6:13-14 reads *"Wherefore take unto you the whole armour of God, that ye may be able to withstand in the evil day, and having done all, to stand. Stand therefore, having our loins gird about with truth, and having on the breastplate of righteousness."* God's word is true and if we can just stand on it, surely He will bring deliverance. It's time to shift again because the RPMs are about to max out…you PRESS your way into 3rd.

You shift to 3rd and the gear opens up the motor a little more. But there is still a little bit of jerking going on…that devil has reared his head again because he thinks you still belong to him. First Corinthians 15:58 reads – *"Therefore, my beloved brethren, be ye stedfast, unmovable, always abounding in the work of the Lord, forasmuch as ye know that your labor is not in vain in the Lord."* The Holy Spirit told me to get busy… that whatever my hands found to do in the ministry…to do it. We had to break the devil's stronghold, so I began searching out my gifts and talents. I worked on as many auxiliaries as I could…I had a lot of idle time on my hands…and I knew I had to stay away from home until bed time, so that when I went home I would be too tired to talk when he called or I wouldn't be tempted to answer the door when he stopped by. Some nights I was so tired, all I could do was roll into the bed. I remained steadfast in using my gifts and talents in the ministry. I knew that if I remained steadfast, surely my trip with God would get a little easier. I found that I had a passion for serving others, so Hospitality became the love of my life. I was ready now…shifting to 4th gear was a breeze.

Shifting into 4th Gear takes us nearer to that place of victory. The devil now knows that you have found the key to breaking his stronghold. He knows that all you have to do is call on the name of Jesus. Most standard shift vehicles have five gears, but some vehicles will allow you to drive a great distance in 4th gear. If there is a 5th gear it is best to shift into that 5th to get the maximum potential from the vehicle. After you have climbed the mountains, gone through the valleys, darted your way through traffic...clear highway is ahead. You can see yourself jumping from 4th to 5th gear...giving God your all. Then you shift...the wind is blowing through your hair, you've opened that engine up all the way...and you can finally see Deliverance Street just up ahead. But before you get there, you come upon a road block. This road block causes you to have to stop, which means that you have to drop the gear to neutral...oops, you find yourself missing the mark again. Valentines Day has arrived and the enemy knows how every woman feels about that day... You get flowers unexpectedly...as a matter of fact...he hand delivers them so that they arrive on time. He calls...wants to take you out to lunch (although the other woman will be taken to dinner later). Suddenly, you shift to "reverse" and make a detour. *"Though he fall, he shall not be utterly cast down, for the Lord upholdeth him with his hand."* If you can only remember, no matter where you've been, no matter what you have done, God is faithful and just...and He will forgive every single sin...pick you up, clean you up and put you right back where you left off. Nobody can do you like Jesus can... NOBODY!! But repentance must take place.

I want you to know that if you have separated yourself from the love of God or fallen short...you yet belong to God. Hosea 14:4 says *"I will heal their backsliding, I will love them freely: for mine anger is turned away from him."* God promises to heal you and He will love you freely if you return to him. His arms are like that 5th gear...wide open and ready to put His shield of protection and love around you. Surrender to Him today, and let Him love all of the hurt away. You may have just gotten in a position where you just don't know how to trust God anymore. Whatever situation you are in, God already knows and He has allowed it for such a time as this...because He knows that you can bear it. He said in His word that He won't put more on us than we can bear. I can't remember if these are words to a song, but I want to share them with you.

I've decided to follow my Savior, I've decided to let Him lead. I've heard the Savior calling. I now accept His Saving Grace. He gives me power to do His Will. He offers strength from day to day. His righteousness is all I need. I open my heart, I hear Him say...no turning back; no turning back.

Believe In Your Seed

Now faith is the substance of things hoped for, the evidence of things not seen. – Hebrews 11:1, KJV

I'm sure you have heard this scripture quoted many times, whether from the pulpit, a radio broadcast, or even from another believer. We also know that without "faith" it is impossible to please God. But where does faith come from? Is it possible to just have faith? In the scripture above, it states that faith is the <u>substance</u> of things hoped for. If faith is considered the substance...or matter, or stuff, or material, then I ask again, where does faith come from? As I was studying on faith some time ago in my quiet time, I found out that we can't get or just have faith...why; because faith is a gift from God and therefore must be planted by God. Romans 10:17 says, *"So then Faith cometh by hearing, and hearing by the word of God."*

I also found in my time of studying that faith begins as a seed, so it is the substance. In order for faith to be produced, you must first have something to believe in...the seed. The seed is the promise, and you just can't believe without the seed. This seed can be planted in your spirit directly from God...through a dream, a prophecy, or word spoken through a mediator. Whatever the case, we can't have it unless God gives it to us, which brings me back to my point of saying that faith is a gift from God and is planted through a seed.

God woke me up at 1:30 a.m. on a Monday morning November 2004 and told me that He had greater things for me in 2005. I began to evaluate my life, where I had been, the sacrifices I had made, the desires I had...then I asked God "What greater things do you have for me, Lord?" I didn't get an answer immediately, but I began living each day in expectancy because 2005 wasn't here yet. In January, I received a call from a lady who didn't know my name, but said the Lord flashed my face before her while in her prayer closet. The Lord charged her to address the "sins of the flesh" during a Women's Conference, but she didn't know who she would get to teach the class. She prayed and asked the Lord to give her someone to teach on the subject.

As He flashed my face before her, she remembered that I had been to some of her meetings and she ran and got the registration sheet on which we had all signed. She asked the Lord to show her who I was because she knew what district I was from. Sure enough, she stated that the Lord highlighted my name before her very eyes. When she called me, I had just stepped away from my desk at work, but she left a message explaining who she was and that she didn't know if she had the right person or not, but that I needed to call her back and she would explain what she wanted.

Now prior to walking away from my desk, I had been on a fast and was praying to the Lord and promising Him that I would do whatever He asked me to do…without any question. I would go wherever He told me to go and say whatever He wanted me to say, when the opportunity arose. I came back to my desk, saw the message light, listened to the message then returned the call. After she explained why she was calling me, I told her that she didn't know what she had just done to me. God had been delivering me from the very thing He needed me to go and teach on…Sins of the Flesh. I couldn't ask, "Why me God," I had just made Him a promise… but ooh, did I ever want to back off of this one! After it was all said and done, this was one of the most awesome conferences I had ever attended. God showed up during the workshop, women were delivered and set free! From that seminar, what God had given to me to deliver to His people was taken back to individual churches and taught in their women's classes.

He said "Greater things." I continued to live in expectancy of what God was going to do because that was in March of that year and I still had nine more months to go. I then received a promotion on my job. During the month of October while sitting in an early service, our Pastor stated that God wasn't through blessing us… those that had an ear heard what the Spirit said to the church. I knew that I was one of those people because God had just told me that this was my season, so I continued to believe in my seed.

On Tuesday, January 31st, I received a call from a colleague of mine from another company in the city. She told me that her old position was open and they wanted her to recommend someone; so she called me and asked for my resume. I sent it to her the following morning. She called me the next day and asked if I had received her email. I told her no and she then stated that I was being asked to come in for an interview. We set the interview up for the next day, Friday. I believed the job was mine because I yet believed God for more. On the following Sunday night, during service, then Prophetess Fannie Marlowe Hightower (Coleman) laid hands on me and two other young ladies and said promotion. After not hearing anything for about four days, I received a phone call from this same friend of mine. She said I have some not so good news… they offered someone else the job. She explained why…and I understood…because I felt like God had something else in store. "I still believed in my seed." She told me that she wanted to forward my resume to another department, and I told her don't hesitate. Within five minutes of hanging up the telephone, I received a call regarding an interview for this new opening.

I was told that my resume was so impressive, they wanted to interview me for not one…but two positions! They explained that they wanted to see which one I was more suitable for. You see, one door was closed, but two were opened…Hallelujah, Glory to God!!! I called my prayer partner, and we prayed before I walked in for the interview; we asked God to make the *crooked places straight* and *to go before me* so that He would be there when I got there. The first interview went extremely well from my end of the room. I knew God was in the place. The second interview from my end was not so well, but I yet believed in my seed.

The next day, I got a phone call from the interviewer. He stated "I'm calling because we were so impressed with you that we would like to offer you the position. You absolutely blew us away during the interview process." He then told me how much they would like to offer, with future benefits to come upon performance. Now, because God was behind all of this…not only did he bless me financially with this position, but He blessed me with a desire of my heart. I obtained the job that I had only dreamt about, and had only volunteered to do in the companies I had worked for.

By faith Noah, being warned of God, moved with fear, prepared an ark to save his house, and became heir of the righteousness which is by faith. Through faith, Sarah received strength to conceive seed, and delivered a child when she was past age, because she judged God faithful who had promised. Now that you know that faith is a gift from God, begin to believe in the seeds He has planted in your life and allow those seeds to be watered and nurtured to produce fruit. God has planted some seeds of faith in your life...now it is time to be obedient to His Will and do just what the Master requires of you.

Who Has the Power?

Let every soul be subject unto the higher powers. For there is no power but of God: the powers that be are ordained of God.

– Romans 13:1

During one Sunday morning worship service, I was turning to the scripture our Pastor asked us to turn to, and while on my way there, this particular verse was magnified before my eyes. As I began to ponder on the scripture and read on a little further...the Lord began to reveal to me how little we realize that the enemy has no power.

It was at this time that I began telling the Lord that no longer will I give place to the devil; no longer will I give credence to the enemy for the valleys I experience along my journey with God. You may wonder how we give the enemy credence or authority for misfortunes or pitfalls...or whatever is going on to make us doubt that God is who He is and that there is another power other than Him. Well, we do that when we call the enemy's name...when we acknowledge his presence, when we give him credit for the things that we are going through. One thing I've found out about God in my walk is that everything we go through, we encounter it because He allows it. He allows it because if we never had any opposition, how could we grow...what would we have to make us stronger...how could our faith in Him be increased? Let me give you a good example from a story a friend shared with me.

There were two engineers who set out to do an experiment on whether trees could thrive or grow deep roots in the desert without wind. One engineer planted his tree in a part of the desert where no winds blew; the other engineer planted his tree in another part of the desert where the winds were really rambunctious. As the tree that was planted in the windy part of the desert was tried and tested by opposing winds...its' roots grew deeper and deeper into the sand, so that it would not get blown away. The roots of the tree that was in the windless part of the desert grew on the surface, because it never faced any opposition.

How many times have we allowed the enemy to snatch something away from us that we said "God gave to us?" How many times have we gone to church, heard the word, danced and shouted, fell out on the alter, then walked out of church only to encounter something or someone along the way that upset us to the point where we wanted to curse...or we did?! So the word never took root.

The time has come for us to stop allowing the enemy to have his way with us. Whether it is in our finances, on our jobs, in our homes, in our relationships...whatever we are going through, we have to realize that God is only allowing us to go through it to make us better; to give us wisdom and understanding of the things life can throw at us. We don't have to give the enemy credit for anything...but all power belongs to God and He has given us the power to declare victory over our lives...in our situations and our circumstances. Ephesians 3:20 reads, *"Now unto him that is able to do exceeding abundantly above all that we ask or think, **according to the power that worketh in us.**"* So let me as you a question, "Who has the power?" Not only does God have the power, but Luke 10:19 tells us: *"Behold, I give unto you power to tread on serpents and scorpions, and over all the power of the enemy: and nothing shall by any means hurt you."* God gives us the power to walk all over the enemy when he tries to rear his ugly head in our lives.

As a matter of fact, you don't even have to acknowledge him... just start speaking the word of God...I can do all things through Christ who strengtheneth me; by His stripes I am healed; or use the word to affirm your faith in the Lord...My times are in His hand and He will care for me and carry all my burdens; the power of God is at work in me; all the precious promises that are Yea and Amen in Christ are mine; I am of God, and am His child, and I have overcome them, because He who is in me is greater than he who is in the world. The enemy only has power when we yield to him and give him the power. I ask you again..."Who has the power?"

Can God Trust You?

Trust in the Lord, and do good; so shalt thou dwell in the land, and verily thou shalt be fed. Delight thyself also in the Lord; and he shall give thee the desires of thine heart. Commit thy way unto the Lord; trust also in him; and he shall bring it to pass. – **Psalms 37:3-5**

Have you ever been in a situation where you were tempted to do something good (righteous) over doing something bad (evil)? I would be willing to say that this is something that happens to us all and more often than we can probably remember. If I had to think about it, I wouldn't have to think long. Let me show you how God will send you a signal before a situation occurs. As a member of this professional organization, we had to meet once a month on a Monday night. During one of these meetings, a young lady I know shared with me that she was ready for a new job; and how her present job was literally driving her nuts and taking away from her family and worship time. I've had opportunities to witness her in action with her job and after knowing her personality, I felt I could certainly keep an eye out for her when positions became available.

On that following Tuesday, I received a call from a well-known company wanting to interview me for a position. My resume had been forwarded to them by a member of my organization. I was overwhelmed with excitement of just the mere thought that God allowed yet another opportunity to come my way. As the young lady began telling me about the job and all the accolades associated with the foundation, my flesh began to get greedy. I then asked how much the position paid. Now how many companies do you know would actually give you the salary range for a position over the telephone? Well guess what, it was given to me and my flesh really began to get greedy. I then realized how blessed I was and how good God had been, and is yet being to me, so I began to rebuke my flesh.

I informed the lady that I had just taken a position with another company and wanted to stick with my decision. She continued to encourage me to come over for the interview and how great a job it would be for me because of my background...I again declined and told her that I felt this was an opportunity for God to bless someone else. She then said, "It sounds like to me that God is taking care of you." She then replied, "If you know of someone that would make a good candidate, would you give me their name and ask them to e-mail me their resume." I said, sure. She thanked me and we hung up. Now what was I supposed to do? Without any hesitation and much excitement, I got on the telephone and called the young lady who shared her situation with me. I began to tell her of the position AND the pay scale to see if she expressed an interest. She gave me her email address, and then I went to lunch. Shortly thereafter, I got a telephone call from another young lady I know, and the first words out of her mouth were, "I need a new job." Okay, can you imagine what I was thinking now???? Well, I shared the same information with her and just asked God to bless the person that this job belongs to, in Jesus' Name...that was all that I could get out of my mouth.

Psalms 37 is a Psalm of David's which contrast the upright person with the wicked person. What I saw in my situation was the need to allow the good to rise above the bad. We all have the two sides operating in us and the side we feed the most is the side that will prevail. Do you have a desire that you want God's Blessings on? If so, can He trust you? Do you desire a husband or a wife? If so, have you prepared yourself for that special someone? Is your business in order? Can He trust you? Men, can you deal with being the provider of your home if for some unforeseen reason your wife couldn't work? Can He trust you? For so many years, I attracted men who were either married or already in what they considered a committed relationship. Yes, I went there because it's happening every day, in and out of the church. We have women up in the church who don't realize how precious they are and don't realize that God has someone especially for them...you don't have to settle for anything less than the best when you are a child of the King. Guess what? If God can't trust you with that special someone, then He won't give you that special someone until you are ready for him or her.

Have you asked God for a new car? Can He trust you enough to give you one? Do you keep the oil changed in the one you have... do you wash it...is it junky inside??? When was the last time you offered someone a ride to church...the grocery store, or to work? Are you one of those who have asked God for a new job? How do you treat the one you have now? Do you come to work on time... do you work while you are there, or is most of your time spent in the breakroom or down the hall shooting the breeze? Do you spend 50% of your day surfing the internet? Can God trust you? What about a new house...or a house period? How do you keep the house or apartment you have now? Could someone drop in at the spur of the moment and find things in order...I'm not just talking about the front, but are the back rooms...bathrooms decent and in order? Can God trust you with bigger and better? How many times have you opened your home to others? Has someone you know needed a place to lay their head and you refused to come forward and say, "You can stay with me until you get yourself together." Can God trust you?

The Lord has called us to be good stewards of the gifts and blessings He has given to us. I believe that poor stewardship is disrespectful to God and just cause for Him to withhold His blessings from us. Through His grace and mercy, He will always allow us time to do the right thing...to commit our ways unto Him. In any given situation, we should ask ourselves, "What would Jesus do?" I know that by doing this, we are offering our ways to God. Trust in the Lord and do good, so that He can trust in you.

Conquering Ungratefulness

I know how to be abased, and I know how to abound; every where and in all things I am instructed both to be full and to be hungry, both to abound and to suffer need.
- Philippians 4:12, KJV

I wonder how long it took Paul to get to this place…the place of contentment. I don't know about you, but I'm not sure if this is an area that I can truly perfect…and although I may never be able to perfect it, I can say that I have come a long way and now know what contentment means. I guess you could say that I have grown up…I'm no longer drinking milk…but I'm able to chew some meat now.

I can remember so vividly one Sunday night at church, we were asked for a sacrificial seed offering of $10.00. Doesn't sound much like a sacrifice does it? Well it is when you have only $16.00 in your wallet to carry you through the entire week. Well, I must have been feeling real good, because my faith kicked in and I gave the $10. I just believed that God would take care of my needs for the week. When the end of the week had come, I had the same $6 dollars in my wallet that I started the week with. Every day of that week, God had a ram in a bush for me. We are encouraged in the Word to not worry, especially about tomorrow. Matthew 6:34a reads, *"Take therefore no thought for the morrow: for the morrow shall take thought for the things of itself."* If we live one day at a time, we can avoid being consumed with worry.

The reason Paul was content is because he could see life from God's point of view. Paul focused on what he was supposed to do and not on what he felt he should have. One day my pastor was singing the song, "I won't complain." As I began to hear the lyrics of this song, I began thinking about all the recent complaints I had been making, such as, not having anything to wear to work. I have a decent sized walk in closet packed with dresses, suits, pants, skirts, blouses, sweaters, shoes, boots, scarves, purses…then in the attic, wardrobe boxes filled with my seasonal clothes. I began to cry to myself… how could I complain about not having anything to wear, when in fact; I never wore the same thing twice in a two to three-week period. I had so many clothes that I had to give away an entire wardrobe. Here I was complaining about not having anything "new" to wear to work when there are people who don't have a change of clothes at all...people with no shoes to wear...no food to eat...no roof over their heads.

Don't get me wrong, I am so grateful for the things that God has given me...but I just had a relapse...forgot or didn't realize that I was complaining. I told you that I haven't perfected this thing. We all have to get to the place where we become ever so grateful for whatever God has given us. If we recognize that there is someone out there with a lot less than what we have, then appreciation can be realized. I look around my home and there are times when it feels so small, but I tell God "Thank You" for my home because I have one. There are those who don't have a home...some live in shelters, while others live on the street...whether by choice or by force, they are yet homeless. There were times when I looked into the freezer and said that I didn't have anything to cook for dinner. Well, I didn't say there wasn't anything in there to cook...I just didn't want what I had. Then I realized that there are people standing in soup-lines waiting on a hot bowl of soup just to get a meal for the day. I guarantee you...those people have a greater appreciation for what they are able to get than those of us who have more. I've realized that contentment is necessary. Paul concentrated on eternal things, not laying his treasures on earth. Where does your perspective lie? What about your priorities?

Even when we are going through the storm and the rain, we are to be content with where God has us, because He promises that trouble won't last always. We know that if He allowed us to enter into the valley, then He can surely deliver us from our valley experiences. When we learn to accept what God allows, then we can conquer ungratefulness.

Do You Want to be Seen?

"Servants, be obedient to them that are your masters according to the flesh, with fear and trembling, in singleness of your heart, as unto Christ; Not with eye service, as menpleasers; but as the servants of Christ, doing the will of God from the heart; With good will doing service, as to the Lord, and not to men: Knowing that whatsoever good thing any man doeth, the same shall he receive of the Lord, whether he be bond or free."

– Ephesians 6:5-8

It seems like every time I sit down to write, my mind starts in one direction, but the Lord directs it another. This passage of scripture simply explains it all to me. There are times when I sit down to write and may not always have heard from the Lord by the time I sit down, but when I do finally sit down, He then takes over and directs me where He would have me to go...and I said He directs... not me. I'm not sure why He wants me to go this way, but I hope that this word will enlighten you as you read it today and give you direction and confirmation in this area of your life.

A few years ago, I went home after a particular service at my church. I'm sure it was during a time when I was serving in ministry in some capacity. I'm sure I've shared somewhere on another day how the Lord spoke to me and told me to get busy...that whatever my hands found to do in ministry...do it! Well, as I said before...I'm almost sure it was in the area of hospitality...serving man. Although I've worked in many areas of the church, this area is of passion to me because it is an area where it created humility within me. It takes a great deal of humbleness to be at the beck and call of another man or woman. To jump when they say jump...run when they say run...bring me this, bring me that...do you know what I mean? Regardless of whether I was serving man or woman, I didn't look at it that way...I was serving in ministry and therefore, I saw it as serving unto God. Not just this area, but there were many areas where I raised my hand and volunteered to do many things...to serve in many areas because I wanted my service to be pleasing to God. Not only was I diligent in my service to the ministry, but I took those qualities into the workplace.

In doing so, I watched as God began to raise me up in ministry and also on my job. I could actually feel and see the favor of God on my life. Not only could I see it, but others began to see it too. That is when the enemy began to get busy and start messing. As I was stating earlier, I went home one day after serving, very disturbed or more so wounded by what I heard others say about me. There were some who even had the audacity to speak things to my face. But what did they know…were they simply jealous because of the favor on my life? What was it? Why did they care? Who was I hurting? She just wants to be seen…said one. Another said, I've been there; done that…you will get tired. Another, Why do you work in so many areas of ministry? As I said, I was a bit wounded from this because I knew in my heart why I was serving with tenacity. It wasn't about them or the people I was serving; it was about me and my Lord.

It was difficult for me to get past this until the Lord woke me up early one morning, and placed this question in my spirit, "Do you want to be seen?" He then began to make some things clear to me…for one, MY PURPOSE and the reason He has called me. He said to me, if you want to be found doing my work, you have to be seen. How do you think Jesus made such an impact in this world? His purpose was to be seen doing the Will of His Father. Although He was 30 years of age when He began His ministry, He still accomplished the purpose He was sent to earth to accomplish, but He could not touch the world if He was never seen. People had to see the Messiah to believe there even was one. How do you think Dr. Martin Luther King impacted this world? He was seen…don't you remember how he stood up for the rights of many? We all have a purpose and we must be seen in order to fulfill that purpose. But make sure that when you are seen, that it is not for show…for the eyes of men (men-pleasers). He said to me, "Show them the joy that I give you down on the inside, show the peace that you've received from me, show love to all of your brothers and sisters. There are so many people who are in need of Me, but you have to get out there to show them and tell them I am yet alive and I am here for them."

So I ask you this question, "How can we impact the world around us if we are not seen?" We can't just read this word…we have to LIVE this word! This Word has to be manifested in our lives. Second

34

Corinthians 3:2-3 says, "**Ye are our epistle written in our hearts, known and read of all men: Forasmuch as ye are manifestly declared to be the epistle of Christ ministered by us, written not with ink, but with the Spirit of the living God; not in tables of stone, but in fleshly tables of the heart**." If it is in us, it will reflect on the outside of us and men will be able to see HIM when they see us. God has strategically placed His chosen people in places where the impact is needed. Do you claim to be one of the called? What about one of the few chosen? If so, are you being seen doing the Will of God? Are you living the life that reflects the image of Christ? When people around you encounter your presence…do they run the other way or are they drawn to the God in you?

I'm going to share this one last story before I close. I believe that we all get some level of satisfaction when we are complimented or told when we have made an impact on someone's life. On my last day at the company I was leaving, I was showered with gifts on top of gifts…some of those gifts came in the form of money. I could not believe how many lives I had impacted by being an employee there. My actions were observed on a daily basis and I had no idea that I was being that closely watched. When the people began to share with me their feelings, I was in tears. I was in tears because I've only been doing what my Father has asked me to do, and I realized that it is what people are looking for and needing everyday.

I won't go into details about what was shared because I don't want it to seem as if I am tooting my own horn…but I live so that others can see God in me. I live so that God can use me. I haven't always been an obedient child…but I try to treat others the way I want to be treated…you know…the Golden Rule. It is my purpose to let my light so shine before men that they may see MY good works and GLORIFY my FATHER which is in Heaven. So the next time a person asks you if you are trying to be seen…tell them yes!

What's Love Got To Do With It?

Thou shalt not avenge, nor bear any grudge against the children of thy people, but thou shalt love thy neighbor as thyself: I am the Lord. - Leviticus 19:18, KJV

With all of the scriptures we can find in the Bible on love, I wonder why it is so hard for us to remember how important and urgent that four letter word 'LOVE' is. I wonder why we can't keep this action word on the forefront of our minds when we encounter situations or a particular individual who has just been an absolute thorn in our side. I'm sure we all know that "to love is the greatest commandment." WOW! When we see the words "thou shalt," it means that God is not asking us...He is telling us. Did you know that your neighbor is not just the person living next door to you? Yeah, you know that next door neighbor who won't keep their yard clean...or your neighbor who is the person in the cubicle next to you who you can't stand at times because they are so negative...always saying ugly things about you and others. Your neighbor is also that ex-boyfriend or girlfriend who broke your heart by cheating on you, or kicking you to the curb after taking you for granted...it is your boss who won't give you that promotion because they are too ignorant or unaware of how much of an asset you are to your department and the company.

We all encounter people in our lives that get on our everlasting nerve, but no matter how much they do to hurt us...we still have to love them. Matthew 5:43 KJV says, "For if we love them which love us, what reward have ye?" There is no reward in loving only the people that love us back, but we are commanded to show charity to the very people who make our guts cringe at the sight of them. I enjoy watching Lifetime movies because many of them are based on true stories. I remember watching this movie about a family who had it all. They were doing really well, but then the husband began to cheat on his wife. He did it so well that she had no idea he was cheating. But then he got beside himself and became blatant with his infidelity. If I remember correctly, the wife found out and decided that she wanted nothing else to do with him. The husband had an accident which paralyzed him for life and because they were still married, she made the decision to take him in and care for him. Now that's love! After all the mess he took her through, she still found enough love to take him in and wipe his nasty behind. But somewhere along the way, she fell in love with another man and decided that to be with him, she would move him in to the home she shared with her paraplegic husband.

Now as much as her husband had done to her...my flesh wanted to say that he got exactly what he deserved. But the truth of the matter is she was wrong. In some ways, the story can be a great depiction of love and forgiveness...the part where she decided to take him home and care for him. But when she began another relationship... she fell into Satan's trap. She began to avenge herself...to punish him for everything he had done to her. The Lord said that vengeance is His. We don't have to worry about those that use or abuse us... God's got our backs...therefore, we must continue in Love. You've heard the saying, "What goes around comes around." Well this is true and that is why we have to be careful how we treat others.

If you have been harboring hate in your heart for another being, then let's pray right now in Jesus name. Father, we come before you this day asking your forgiveness for not being obedient to your word. You COMMANDED us to love our neighbor as we love ourselves and sometimes Lord we find that hard to do. God, please forgive us for we know not what we do when we don't allow your word to manifest in our hearts, minds, and souls; but today Lord, we want to start all over. From this day forward Lord, we will love our enemies; we will bless them that curse us; we will do good to them that hate us and hate on us, and we will pray for them who despitefully use us and persecute or discriminate against us, for we want to be your child Lord and represent you.

We want to grow in your spirit and allow you to shine in our lives like never before. Father, give us the wisdom to understand your word and to follow righteousness everyday and we will be ever mindful to give you the praise. Heavenly Father, please don't let a day go by without reminding us of the love you had for us when you allowed your son to be the sacrifice for OUR sins. If we can just remain focused on that alone God, we know that ALL things are possible. All this we ask in your precious son Jesus' name, Amen. Now, what's love got to do with it....EVERYTHING. For God SO

LOVED the world that He gave His only begotten Son...and His Son gave EVERYTHING (His life) for us.

If You Are Not Growing...Check Your Fertilizer!

That we should no longer be children, tossed to and fro and carried about with every wind of doctrine, by the trickery of men, in the cunning craftiness of deceitful plotting, but, speaking the truth in love, may grow up in all things into Him who is the head – Christ – from whom the whole body, joined and knit together by what every joint supplies, according to the effective working by which every part does its share, causes growth of the body for the edifying of itself in love.

– Ephesians 4:14-16, NKJV

God, I'm so tired...I'm so very tired. Lord, I'm so sick and tired of myself not getting it right. I should know by now that this is wrong...as many times as I have been in this place, I should know how the enemy is going to deceive me. But God, he knows just what to say to get me to turn my back on you. He knows just what to do to cause me to fall. God I'm too old for this. I've been in this situation too many times not to get it right by now. I didn't want to go to that party, but I just couldn't let my friend go by him/herself. I know how they like to party and I know how I used to be when I was really out there...somehow I knew that I would end up taking a drink...then another...and another. It won't hurt this one time to go and let her read my palm. It can't hurt...can it? What harm could that be to let someone look into my hand and tell me what they see? Oh boy, that ensemble sure looked good in that window display! I promise you Lord, I won't spend another dime of my bill money...I will make sure to take out my tithes first the very next check I get; I need that outfit! It is just what I've been looking for.

Can you say that you were in one of the above places at one time or another in your life? What about now...where are you now? I ask because it is imperative to realize that the word of God is here to increase us...not decrease us. Day after day, week after week, we hear the Word...through the radio, over the pulpit at church during Sunday morning worship or weekly bible study, or we pick up the bible and read it. How much has the Word you've heard caused you to grow? If you are not growing, you need to check your fertilizer...what you are being fed...your surroundings.

Fertilizer is used on living foliage…plants and trees to increase its possibility for healthy maturity and growth. Fertilizer causes the seeds in a cotton patch to RISE UP and produce balls of cotton… that in turn have purpose…material for clothing. Fertilizer causes dead grass to come to LIFE and form new and thicker patches of grass. Fertilizer simply produces FRUIT!

If you were a habitual liar, the WORD of God (fertilizer) should cause you to put away your lying tongue and speak the truth. If you are quick to get angry, fertilizer will allow you to be angry but sin not. If you were a thief, your fertilizer would cause you to stop stealing and get out and find employment. If you always talked about others negatively when you opened your mouth, your fertilizer should cause you to change your language and speak only those things which are edifying and that ministers healing to those who hear it. If you were a fornicator, your fertilizer should cause you to live free of fleshly sins. None of us are perfect, but I believe that it makes God really proud of us when He can see FRUIT in us. Ephesians 5:8-10 KJV says, "**For ye were sometimes darkness, but now are ye light in the Lord: walk as children of light: (For the fruit of the Spirit is in all goodness and righteousness and truth;) proving what is acceptable unto the Lord.** The bible even goes on to tell us that we should have no fellowship with the unfruitful works of darkness, but rather reprove or rebuke them…tell them the truth.

Who are you keeping company with? Who is in your circle of friends? What are you being fed through them? It is hard sometimes to let go of things and people that keep us tied to darkness, but until we can do that…we will wither away because our fertilizer is expired. How do you know when your fertilizer has taken affect? You will say NO to the things or people who have kept you tied to sin. Your fertilizer is effective when you can see FRUIT…love, joy, peace, longsuffering, gentleness, goodness, faith, meekness, and temperance. If you have realized that growth has not taken place in you…go back and check your fertilizer.

Bringing Things into Perspective

We are troubled on every side, yet not distressed; we are perplexed, but not in despair; Persecuted, but not forsaken; cast down, but not destroyed; Always bearing about in the body the dying of the Lord Jesus, that the life also of Jesus might be made manifest in our body. - 2 Corinthians 4:8-10, KJV

When you take a look at the above passage of scriptures, what are you feeling? What does it say to you? These are words from the BIBLE…yes words letting us know that we are going to have some rainy days, some hard times, some crying, suffering, heartache and pain…but it is how you receive these situations that determines your end result.

A pessimistic person is one who never sees the positive side of things. Not only are they negative, but they are cynical…mocking, distrustful, sarcastic…If they are in debt…they feel they will always be in debt, so they continue to incur debt without ever paying anything off. If they are sick in their body, you can see it on their face. If you had a glass of water…and you drank half of it…a pessimistic person would see a half empty glass.

I believe many of us are faced with some major obstacles in our lives. We've looked back over the years and thought we had gotten past some of those things…but they seemed to just follow us right on into the next year. You may be one of those who are considering a divorce because of your present situation or one going through a major financial battle…pretty much at the point of losing the roof over your head or losing your transportation. You may be one whose transportation is on its last leg and you don't know how you are going to replace it. Along with all of these troubles, the enemy will begin to put things before us that may tempt us to do something outside of the Will of God.

God says in His word, "There hath no temptation taken you but such as is common to man: BUT God is faithful, who will not suffer you to be tempted above that ye are able; but will with the temptation also make a way to escape, that ye may be able to bear it." (1 Corinthians 10:13). God's word says that even though we will be faced with some trouble, we don't have to be distressed...look at the word 'distressed'. When we are distressed, we are unhappy, upset, distraught, worried, anxious, and bothered. His word goes on to say that even though we may be perplexed...puzzled...at a loss...confused...Lord, how did this happen to me? I was so careful this time; we don't have to be in despair...hopeless...in misery... depressed...desolate. Even when people persecute or harass us, we are not forsaken...why? Because He said that He will never leave us nor forsake us. God is always here for us. Even when we have been cast down, just plain ole' thrown away by others, we are not destroyed.

An Optimist is a person who sees a glass half full. They are idealist or romantic...loving, passionate...tender. Optimistic people always look for the good in others because they know there is some good in everyone. An optimistic person will believe that no matter what I am going through, God is able to bring me out of it. Not only do they wait patiently for God to take them through their situation, they go through it with a smile on their face, praise on their lips, thanksgiving in their heart, and worship in their spirit. We can't forget who God is and what He is able to do. Bring the things you are going through into perspective. If you've been looking at your situation through the eyes of a pessimist...STOP! See your situation through optimistic eyes and know that it is coming to an end soon, and when it does...we will see Jesus manifested through you.

A Recipe for Success

And keep the charge of the Lord thy God, to walk in his ways, to keep his statutes, and his commandments, and his judgments, and his testimonies, as it is written in the law of Moses, that thou mayest prosper in all that thou doest, and withersoever thou turnest thyself: That the Lord may continue his word which he spake concerning me, saying, If thy children take heed to their way, to walk before me in truth with all their heart and with all their soul, there shall not fail thee (said he) a man on the throne of Israel.

- 1 Kings 2:3-4

While on his death bed, David was able to give words of wisdom to his son Solomon (otherwise known as the wisest man to ever live). As David's rule was coming to an end, he knew that he needed to reveal to his son the promises the Lord had made to him. Now Solomon didn't just inherit wisdom even though his father was a wise man also, but he asked it of the Lord. He knew that he had some great shoes to fill in coming behind his father and he knew that he had only one place to go to in search of what he needed to be successful...GOD.

Matthew 6:33 tells us "But seek ye first the kingdom of God, and His righteousness; and all these things shall be added unto you." See, Solomon was even wise when he first decided to go to God to ask for wisdom. He didn't wait until he was on the throne for thirty years...doing his own thing...living his life in sin...as most of us do. I can remember so vividly how I used to sit up in church as a teen...hearing the Lord calling out to me to come unto Him. I would answer Him...but it wasn't the answer He wanted to hear. I would say to the Lord, "I'm not ready...I want to live a little of this life...I want to see what is out there...I want to experience some of the things that the world has to offer...God if I come now, I won't stay...I'll just be back on the altar every Sunday getting saved every week...look at the others God, they get saved on Sunday, and sin on Monday and are back on the altar the next time we are in church... God, I don't want to be like that...I don't want to be a hypocrite... wait on me God...please wait on me...I promise when I come Lord,

I won't turn back."

Have you ever thought about where you would be had you established a true relationship with God a long time ago? Look at where you are now...are you prosperous...can you witness to the great things the Lord has done for you...do you have a testimony? Think about where you would have been had that relationship with God started sooner. How much more could you have? Where would you be right about now? You think you have done great things, but greater things you could have done had you heeded the call sooner. Well, those days are gone and a new day has arrived. You may not be exactly where you need to be in God. If you aren't, then now is the time to seek Him while He may be found. We can't find ourselves waiting on God...because if we are waiting on Him...He may never show Himself to us. His word tells us to "seek" Him.

God allowed me to stay out there alright, but the devil almost killed me. He sought for my life...he saw what God was going to do in my life and He wanted to take me out before I could seek the Lord. When the enemy came to take my life...I called out to the Lord, and He heard me. I experienced many things in the world...probably not as much as some others have...and because of His Grace and Mercy, I have a right to go home with the Lord. I've got the enemy under my feet and that is where I am going to keep him!

God's word gives us all kinds of recipes on righteous living and believe it or not, none of those recipes are hard...they just require obedience for proper preparation. Obedience is the key ingredient to seeing God at His return. In all that we do, we should keep this ingredient at the forefront of our minds and remember that God requires it of us.

Ask God for New Vision

And he (Moses) said, I beseech you, shew me thy glory. And he said, I will make all my goodness pass before thee, and I will proclaim the name of the Lord before thee; and will be gracious to whom I will be gracious, and will shew mercy on whom I will shew mercy. And he said, Thou canst not see my face, for there shall no man see me, and live. And the Lord said, Behold, there is a place by me, and thou shalt stand upon a rock: And it shall come to pass, while my glory passeth by, that I will put thee in a clift of the rock, and will cover thee with my hand while I pass by: And I will take away mine hand, and thou shalt see my back parts: but my face shall not be seen. - Exodus 33:18-23

Can you step back a moment and think about what Moses could have been thinking when he asked the Lord to show him HIS Glory??? I could just hear God saying…WHAT! Moses you can't handle me! You know why you can't handle me? Because if you saw my face, you would have to die! Are you ready for that Moses? Are you? Let me answer that for you…NO! Why, because if you are dead, then you are of no use to me. I need you alive because I have purpose for you and you can't do the things I have for you to do if you are dead. Yes, I can get someone else to complete the task, but I CHOSE you and you alone. You better be careful what you ask for!

Although Moses didn't get to see God's face, he got closer to God's Glory, or he got more anointing. It was after this that Moses began to seek from God new vision. Later in Chapter 34, verses 5-9 God reveals the new vision to Moses, *"And the LORD descended in the cloud, and stood with him there, and proclaimed the name of the LORD. And the LORD passed by before him, and proclaimed, The LORD, The LORD God, merciful and gracious, longsuffering, and abundant in goodness and truth, Keeping mercy for thousands, forgiving iniquity and transgression and sin, and that will by no means clear the guilty; visiting the iniquity of the fathers upon the children, and upon the children's children, unto the third and to the fourth generation. And Moses made haste, and bowed his head toward the earth, and worshipped. And he said, If now I have found grace in thy sight, O Lord, let my Lord, I pray thee, go among us; for it is a stiff-necked people; and pardon our iniquity and our sin, and take us for thine inheritance."*

God knew what He was doing by choosing Moses. Moses was an intelligent man, even though he had low self-esteem in the early years before his calling, God knew what Moses was made of, and so He knows what we are made of. Some of us are walking around with stale visions, old ways of doing things, driving the same old route to work every day without seeking out a new or even better route, we've let dreams die because we never pursued God's way of bringing them to pass. Man of God, Woman of God, do you not know your purpose, your destiny!????? God has already revealed some things to you for you to do, but you haven't pursued the vision. That is okay. You don't have to worry because you can ask God now for "New Vision," just as Moses did.

Ask God to show you His Glory! Ask God to show Himself anew; to open your eyes of faith to Him. Now, if you are not going to do anything with the new vision, then don't open your mouth and waste your time or God's by asking. God is looking for a people who will do what He tells them to do, say what He tells them to say, and go where He tells them to go. It is only when we accept the task that He gives to us, that His Glory can be revealed in and to us. Moses petitioned the Lord for the people because they were stiff-necked, hard headed folk! God had to shower down Grace and Mercy to cover these people. He does the same for us each and every day. It is a wonder some of us are still alive today after all that we have done. But the reason we are alive is to fulfill the vision of the Lord, so that we may minister to those who need to be ministered to. Yes, there may be someone around you who needs to see the light of God's vision illuminating around you. That illumination should be the Glory of God...and when they see it, they will want it.

When God's anointing is in the place, it destroys the yoke, burdens, oppression, and bondage. If you have it (the anointing), praise God because the vision should be clearer to you, and you should be doing great things in the name of Jesus. If you don't, don't be afraid, just do what Moses did, ask God for 'New Vision'.

Taking Full Responsibility

"You have heard that the Law of Moses says, 'If an eye is injured, injure the eye of the person who did it. If a tooth gets knocked out, knock out the tooth of the person who did it' But I say, don't resist an evil person! If you are slapped on the right cheek, turn the other, too. If you are ordered to court and your shirt is taken from you, give your coat, too. If a soldier demands that you carry his gear for a mile, carry it two miles. Give to those who ask, and don't turn away from those who want to borrow." Matthew 5:38-42, NLT

"Come on Jesus...You want me to do what? Oh no, you can't expect that of me..."

Have you ever heard the saying, "for every action there is a reaction?" Every time one person commits an act (and we will say wrongful act) against another person, it causes that person to retaliate or seek retribution for what just happened to them. In most cases, the person seeking retribution normally causes greater harm to the other than what they experienced. I know you know what I am talking about...especially if you were ever a teen. I've learned that there is a small gap between the stimulus (the agent that influences the action) and the reaction (the end result of the stimulus' influence). Are you with me? Keep that in mind...because we will come back to that.

When was the last time you allowed someone's action to cause you to react...most importantly, in a negative way? Think about that for a moment. Was it your spouse, a child, your co-worker, someone in traffic, or your boss? How did it make you feel on the inside? Did it make you want to lash out verbally...how about physically?

The time it takes for you to react to the stimulus that caused you to get upset is what's known as the "Gap." Did you know that you have the ability to widen the gap that lies between the stimulus of your emotions and your reaction to the stimulus? You can either allow that gap to be increased or decreased. If that gap is decreased, it results in a person with a short fuse...or you might say…a bomb ready to explode! OR you can make a conscious decision to increase that gap. You can increase that gap by keeping control of the situation and not reacting to it in a negative way. You might think this is hard…and it may be in some extreme situations; but if you think about it, when you give someone else control in your situation, you lose power…with no power…you have no influence…and if you have no influence…you have no control. If you can't influence anyone…what good are you? God has called us all to be World Changers; we can't change the world if we have no influence…no power…or no control over our own lives and situations. You might ask…how can I regain control? You gain control of your situation by taking 100% responsibility. There are some things in this life that you just have no control over…but the one thing you have control over is "your individual response."

Yes, 100% responsibility says that, "I am 100% responsible for how I choose to respond to the enemy and circumstances in my life…and everyone else is 0% responsible. Do you think Jesus was teaching us this for no reason? He obviously gave us the ammunition to win our wars. We don't have to fight our own battles. I will give you a perfect example. I went through a situation at a previous employer in which I could have lost my job. There are some evil people in this world…and I'm sure you know of a few. While in that situation, I tried to fight for my rights and take up for myself because I knew that what they were trying to do to me wasn't right. Every time I squirmed…it dug me deeper and deeper into a hole with these people. I tried to move out of the department…I got blackballed. But then God sent the word for me to do exactly the opposite of what they (the stimulus) expected me to do. After I was blackballed, my next step was to file a grievance…God said, "be still and know that I am God. Come to work…be quiet…do your job…don't say anything unless I free you to say it." Yes, that messed me up.

Inadvertently, the "gap" of my reaction to the stimulus was increased by being obedient to what I heard the Lord say. The evil doers began to question what was going on with me. "You mean to tell me she is not going to fight us…what you say!!!? This can't be right…this is not what we expected her to do. Let's keep an eye on her." Months began to pass by as I waited on the victory (because it was sure to come)…I was keeping peace with all men.

I was eventually promoted out of the department. To make a long story short, a few years later a "transformation" took place…one person was moved out of their position, and eventually took early retirement; another person's sickness came back upon them, two other's were asked to leave the company, and the only one left apologized for what happened. Don't get me wrong, I take no glory from their tribulation…but you can't mess with God's people! He does not play!!! Didn't He say that vengeance is His? Didn't He say that He would fight your battles? Didn't He? As long as I tried to control my situation, that situation took control of me…but when my response became "Yes, Lord…I will do what you say"…God took control. I no longer had any control, power, or influence, but God allowed me to see the manifestation of His power some years later.

I'm sure you've heard this as well as I have…that married couple's share responsibility, 50/50…but in essence…it is 100% responsibility from both ends. I guarantee that it will make for a better marriage. If you are single, please consider that if you are thinking about getting married. Sometimes petty words can cause a couple to go to bed angry, but when each person takes responsibility for what they say and how they react…it will make for a better relationship. I believe God is calling us to greater accountability. He desires for us to take full responsibility of our actions. He's removing the excuses for why we choose to act or respond inappropriately. It's up to us to take heed. And Jesus said, "Anyone who listens to my teaching and obeys me is wise, like a person who builds a house on solid rock. But anyone who hears my teaching and ignores it is foolish like a person who builds a house on sand." Matthew 7:24 & 26 NLT

Wearing Jesus

Jesus Christ the same yesterday, and to day, and for ever.
- Hebrews 13:8, KJV

Do you remember the season of the WWJD? I'm talking about the period when it seemed as if everyone was purchasing and wearing WWJD items such as bracelets, photo frames, necklaces, t-shirts, earrings, bumper stickers, and paper weights...remember...the What Would Jesus Do paraphernalia? It even seemed as if the world had jumped on the WWJD bandwagon. A bandwagon is simply a movement...a series of activities working toward an objective that attracts growing support. The maker or creator who designed the acronym WWJD, he or she had a purpose. I would be safe to say that their purpose was more than likely to get as many people as possible to ponder this question in their mind in the midst of temptation; in the midst of trials and tribulation...to ask themselves, "What Would Jesus Do?"

Did this not challenge you to consider God when trying to make a decision...to examine your life by His standards? When we are in wilderness moments, and we don't know where to go, what to do, how to do it, or when...we should be like David in Psalms 63:1 "O God, thou art my God; early will I seek thee: my soul thirsteth for thee, my flesh longeth for thee in a dry and thirsty land, where no water is." When we give Jesus authority over our lives, we are saying to Him, I belong to you, Lord, I believe in you, and I am going to put Your Will before my will. I won't move left nor right without hearing from you God....whatever you tell me to do, I will do. Not my will but Thy Will be done. We can't wear Jesus on our wrist; we can't wear Him on our head, and neither around our necks, but the only place that we can wear Jesus is in our hearts. If He is worn in our hearts, then He will appear on the outside of us...where others can see Him. They will see Him by the way we treat others. They will see Him by the way we carry ourselves. Remember, a tree is known by the fruit it bears. Doesn't it make you stand up tall to be sporting Jesus...for others to see what a change that has taken place in your life?

That's how I feel now…to know that all of my past is just that…the past. It doesn't matter what folks think of me when they hear about my past, because "What did Jesus Do"…He forgave me of all of my iniquities; and that is why I'm not ashamed of my past…because I have a future and I have Hope. When you wear Jesus, even your enemies will be at peace.

We must wear Jesus at all times…and not just in items purchased with money…but wear Him in our hearts…wear Him by how we treat others…wear Him by being Holy…wear Him by showing love to those in need. He should be seen in our lives every day. Many of us will be the only Jesus some people see…so wear Jesus well! When the enemy tries to tempt you…WWJD? "Get thee hence, Satan. For it is written, Thou shalt worship the Lord thy God, and him only shalt thou serve" Matthew 4:10. When people persecute you, WWJD? Jesus would, "Rejoice, and be exceeding glad; for great is your reward in heaven", Matthew 4:12a. When someone despitefully use you, WWJD? "Pray for them".

Jesus Christ is the same, yesterday, today and forever. Wearing Jesus should never be just a phase or a season in our lives, as the paraphernalia representing Jesus was…He is here for us through every season. We should always consider the things we do and consequences behind those decisions. Always…in everything that concerns you…ask yourself the question "What Would Jesus Do?" When we are positively affecting the world around us…then we will know that we are wearing Jesus.

What Do You Have To Fear?

The Lord is my light and my salvation; whom shall I fear? The Lord is the strength of my life; of whom shall I be afraid? When the wicked, even mine enemies and my foes, came upon me to eat up my flesh, they stumbled and fell. Though an host should encamp against me, my heart shall not fear: though war should rise against me, in this will I be confident. One thing have I desired of the Lord, that will I seek after; that I may dwell in the house of the Lord all the days of my life, to behold the beauty of the Lord and to enquire in his temple. – Psalms 27:1-4, NKJV

As I was reading this chapter of Psalms, I began to think about the author, David and how great a conqueror he was. David...a Shepherd, a warrior, a musician, an outlaw, a faithful friend, an empire builder, a sinner, a saint, a failed father, an ideal king! Who, but David could write such anointed words of appreciation to God? David was a fearless man...one who had killed lions, bears... and even the giant Goliath. He feared nothing and nobody. He feared no one but God. David wasn't crazy...he knew where his strength lay...in spite of his many faults, he was a man after God's own heart.

Although the word fear is a small word...it is one that has great impact if it's allowed to slip its way into our hearts and minds. Fear originates in the mind. It exists to discourage the believer from receiving the blessings of God. Fear is simply a tactic of the devil. The enemy uses it to keep us from moving forward...from getting all that God has for us. Fear can entrap you; it will deceive you; it will cause us to be apprehensive about things, events or situations in our lives, when there is no need to be.

There are two forms of fear: secular (worldly) fear and religious (spiritual) fear. Secular fear arises in the normal activities and relationships of life. We as humans fear other humans, we fear animals...we are afraid of death, of disaster, of being overtaken by adversity or hardships and by all means afraid of the unknown. Fear can reflect the limitations of life, as well as, the unforeseen consequences of actions. Fear can be the honor a child demonstrates toward his or her parents. Fear also comes because of the consequences of sin or from a strong awareness or realization of sin and disobedience. Remember Adam and Eve in the garden? Gen 3:9-10, "And the Lord God called unto Adam, and said unto him, Where art thou? And he said, I heard thy voice in the garden, and I was afraid, because I was naked; and I hid myself." Abimelech was afraid when he realized that he had committed an offensive act by taking Sarah, the wife of Abraham as his wife (Gen. 20:8-9). This sense of separation and guilt that comes as consequence of sin produces in the heart of individuals the fear of the day of the Lord, because we will appear before the judgment of God. This is an example of religious fear. To fear God is the beginning of wisdom.

Freedom from fear comes as we trust in God, who protects and helps us. There is no fear in love; but perfect love casteth out fear: because fear hath torment. He that feareth is not made perfect in love. (1 John 4:18). We are no longer slaves of fear because God has not given us the spirit of fear, but the spirit of power, love, and a sound mind (II Tim 1:7). I realize that not fearing is easier said than done, but we have to remember who God is and we can't live our lives as prisoners of fear.

I heard a very profound quote one day, while watching the movie "Akeelah and the Bee." Prior to hearing this insightful statement during the movie, I heard it one other time at a conference. After hearing it the second time, I went in search of it on the internet and found the actual quote...word for word. And it reads,

> *"Our deepest fear is not that we are inadequate. Our deepest fear is that we are powerful beyond measure. It is our light, not our darkness that most frightens us. We ask ourselves, Who am I to be brilliant, gorgeous, talented, fabulous? Actually, who are you not to be? You are a child of God. Your playing small does not serve the world. There is nothing enlightened about shrinking so that other people won't feel insecure around you. We are all meant to shine, as children do. We were born to make manifest the glory of God that is within us. It is not just in some of us; it is in everyone. And as we let our own light shine, we unconsciously give other people permission to do the same. As we are liberated from our own fear, our presence automatically liberates others."*
> *by Marianne Williamson*

Allow these words to marinate in your mind and heart. Then remember to set yourself free from your fears, so that God can do in you what He desires to do. You are the key to someone's blessing… you've held back you input on the job long enough; your opinion matters. Share that insight. If you feared applying for the job opening simply because you didn't get the last position you applied for, shake that off and apply for the job you really want. Is it your desire to start your own business? What do you have to fear? God is waiting on you to take one step so that He can take two. Have you been afraid to love again…to let go of the hurt? I've learned to love as if I've never been hurt before. It is the only way to receive the love God has for you. Thinking about going back to school… but don't think that your brain can handle it? Go ahead, step out on faith…what do you have to fear?

A Sacrifice of Praise

Therefore I will praise you, O LORD, among the nations; I will sing praises to your name. He gives his king great victories; he shows unfailing kindness to his anointed, to David and his descendants forever. - II Samuel 22:50-51, NKJV

Have you ever been so inundated with your problems that all you did was complain to God in your time of prayer? Well today, this is your opportunity to put your problems aside. Today is the day you won't trouble God with your problems. If you've been perplexed with the issues of life, why don't you take the time today to offer up a sacrifice of praise. I too have days when I just don't feel like getting out of bed...could be a spirit of depression...could be just plain laziness, but whatever the case...if God sees fit to allow me to open my eyes, then I need to Thank and Praise Him for His Goodness and His Mercy towards me.

I'm like David, there is no gift I have that God didn't bless me with. I can do nothing of my own power, but it's the power of God that dwells in me which gives me the ability to perform the task and duties necessary for the day at hand. He is the one who keeps me from dangers seen and unseen. He keeps me sane in times when I feel I should have lost my mind. And so I am encouraged as David was in Psalms 18:2-3 to offer praise unto the Lord. "The Lord is my rock, and my fortress, and my deliverer; the God of my rock; in Him will I trust; He is my shield, and the horn of my salvation, my high tower, and my refuge, my savior, thou savest me from violence. I will call on the Lord, who is worthy to be praised, so shall I be saved from mine enemies"

Before God can move on my behalf...He has to know that I appreciate Him for the things He has already done...that I don't take Him for granted. I can give Him the fruit of my lips; tell Him how much I adore Him and appreciate Him for the things He has done in my life. Even in the midst of going through the storm, He is yet my deliverer and because He is, I know that there is victory on the other side. There is nothing too hard for my God to work out and I will continue to praise and magnify His name. He is worthy, He is magnificent, He is awesome, and I adore Him.

I'm sure that while I am giving Him praise, you are too. I am confident in knowing that there is somebody else feeling the Lord the way I do...someone who gives thought to the things that the Lord has already done in your life. Thank you for taking the time to praise Him with me.

Heed the Warning Signs

And the same day, when the even was come, he saith unto them,
Let us pass over unto the other side. And when they had sent away
the multitude, they took him even as he was in the ship. And there
were also with him other little ships. And there arose a great storm
of wind, and the waves beat into the ship, so that it was now full.
- Mark 4:35-37, KJV

Isn't it amazing how God will allow warning to come just before the
storm?   Well, He did say in His word, that warning comes before
destruction." Think about a natural storm for a moment. What
are some of the warning signs that alert you a storm is coming?
Aren't there dark clouds, straight-line winds, raging seas, thunder
and lightning flashes, and sometimes even hail...right?   What
about warning signs that your finances are about to experience a
storm such as, the alternator playing out on your car, or the starter
going bad...both of which could set you back a pretty penny if they
had to be replaced. What about a storm on the home front? You
play detective and go on an investigative search in your 15 year old
child's bedroom and find condoms, or you read their diary and find
out that the child you thought you knew...you don't know at all.
Maybe a storm has arisen in your marriage and for some reason...
you just didn't pay attention to all of the warning signs. There may
even be a storm on your job...your company has decided to close
their doors and you haven't prepared yourself for the transition.
All of the signs were there, you just didn't take heed.

My desire is to emphasize how powerful God's warning signs are
and how important it is for us to be linked into the spirit so that
we can hear what the spirit is saying when He speaks. Do I need
to remind you that God still speaks to his people...at least those
with an ear to hear what the spirit is saying? One day the Holy
Spirit spoke to me and said, "A storm is coming." After hearing
that, the spirit brought back to my remembrance the above passage
of scripture. I thought He dropped that for me to write about that
day. That was not God's purpose...His purpose was point blank to
warn me that a storm was on its way and I was the prime target. So
on the following Sunday morning, when the Pastor gave his text, I

was in awe...and saying to myself...that really was you God. So as the message went on...I kept thinking to myself that all is well with me. I am almost debt free (thank you Lord for sending me a money manager); my kids are doing fine...strong and healthy (thank you Lord again); I have a new job that's very rewarding (thank you Lord three times over); my mother who had been in the hospital was finally being released from the hospital (I praise you God for your Grace and Mercy)...nothing was coming to mind that He could have been warning me about.

Then I thought, okay God...when all is well and I least expect it... the storm could hit anywhere and at anytime. I thought about Hurricane Katrina and how that storm had no respect of person. It hit the rich as well as the poor. It claimed sinners as victims as well as Christians...Pastor's lost their churches and parishioners were displaced. It was the aftermath of the storm that caused many to perish. They were warned that the levy wouldn't hold...but no one heeded the warning, and so many perished. Considering that, I began to pray and ask the Lord to prepare me for whatever storm was coming my way. It doesn't matter who you are, where you live, how God is using you; when the storm comes and your name is on it...you had better be prepared to endure until it ends. No storm comes into our lives to stay, they will pass. When it's your due season for a storm...endure hardship as a good solder of Jesus Christ (II Timothy 2:3). We can't be like the disciples who panicked when they were on the Sea of Galilee.

When Noah was warned of the flood to come, he obeyed God and built the ark. Mankind was sent warning time, after time, after time, after time...but to no avail, the word went unheeded. God released the flood and it destroyed the earth. Shortly before the fiery destruction of Sodom and Gomorrah, God sent warning to Lot to leave, but he didn't heed the warning at first and chose to linger behind. The bible says that God being merciful to him (Genesis 19:16), caused two angels to drag Lot and his family outside of the city. Had Lot heeded the first warning, his wife may have survived. These are just a couple of examples of warnings given in the bible, some were heeded and some went unheeded.

Storms are situations that cause great anxiety. We can either trust God and His ability to keep us during the storm, or we can panic, fail the test, and endure the next stormy situation in our lives. If God sends warning that a storm is coming (and He usually does), then we must take heed and brace ourselves for it. The warnings are only signals that God is mindful of us and that He doesn't want anything to catch us off guard...and because of this...we can have confidence that He is more than able to get us through them. Even when the waves are raging and it appears that we are about to go under...we have to "know" that it won't consume us...it won't take us out of here...because God is still in control.

If you are currently going through a storm...don't panic! No matter what stormy situations arise, I know God is able to bring you through it victoriously!

Run to Win

Remember that in a race everyone runs, but only one person gets the prize. You also must run in such a way that you will win. All athletes practice strict self control. They do it to win a prize that will fade away, but we do it to win an eternal prize. So I run straight to the goal with purpose in every step. I'm not like a boxer who misses his punches. I discipline my body like an athlete training it to do what it should. Otherwise, I fear that after preaching to others, I myself might be disqualified.

– 1 Corinthians 9:24-27, NLT

What do you tell the teen who thinks they need to run out and purchase the latest Nike shoe every time the latest and greatest shoe hits the market…or the late night shopper who flicks through each paid advertising channel, including HSN and QVC compulsively ordering things they don't need? What about that man or woman who defines sex as their ultimate means of release…or that obese person you know who eats, and eats, and eats like there is no tomorrow? Don't mention the person who likes to gossip about others…as if they are the only one who has a life. Think about this for a moment: If someone were to pay you 5 cent for every kind word you spoke and then collect 5 cent from you for every unkind word…would you be rich or poor? Let that soak in for a moment.

All of the above scenarios are examples of individuals with NO self-control. Not only does self-control play a major role when it comes to an intimate relationship between a man and a woman who are not married, self-control is necessary for all areas of our life. Wouldn't it be easy if the answer to all of these questions was a simple; JUST SAY NO?! Isn't it easy to tell someone to say NO when you haven't walked a mile in their shoes…when you don't understand the reason behind their compulsive actions…when you have no clue as to why there is no self-control in these areas of their lives?

In the above scripture, Paul talks about how in a race there is only one winner. This is true in the natural…but in the spiritual… everyone can be the winner. Verse 24b says, "You ALSO must run in such a way that you MAY WIN." How? By practicing self-control, by living holy, by obeying the Word of God, by looking unto Jesus, the author and finisher of your faith. Temperance is one of the fruit of the Spirit and without it...we won't make it. Then he says, "All athletes practice strict self-control." Here are a couple of key words, first "practice," which means to perform, apply, follow, or observe. I know the Bible is filled with corrupt people...but it also has role models, mentors, and examples. Jesus, along with Paul are two good examples of a role model and mentor. Jesus wouldn't tell you to do something that He was not willing to do himself. Neither did Paul...as he said, "I discipline my body like an athlete, 'training' it to do what it SHOULD." He said "my body," not just his tongue (saying things he shouldn't say, talking about folks he shouldn't be talking about), or his hands (touching places where they shouldn't touch-on him or anyone else, accidentally picking up things that doesn't belong to him), giving his body to someone that is not his. Another key word is "strict" meaning severe, firm, stern, or harsh. Have you ever watched a football player practice? Before they go onto the field, they have to take on some rigorous training. They throw themselves into these huge bean bags while they attempt to push it backwards. They have to be able to take the hit as well as give it. And it takes discipline, which is another key word. It means regulation, order, control, restraint, obedience, taking authority over yourself, your mind, body and your actions...hey, don't forget the tongue.

Paul was a great teacher and encourager. He encouraged the people to persist constantly, diligently, and vigorously in their course. He was letting them know that there was room for them all to get the prize. Keep this in mind; you can not fail if you run well. My goal now is to lay my treasures in heaven where moth and dust does not corrupt, nor thieves break in and steal...My goal is Heaven...I want to go to Heaven; don't you? Then let's run to win.

<u>Seed that Falls on Good Ground</u>

But the good soil represents those who hear and accept God's message and produce a large harvest – [some] thirty, [some] sixty, and even a hundred times as much as had been planted. Then Jesus asked them, "Would anyone light a lamp and then put it under a basket or under a bed to shut out the light? Of course not! A lamp is placed on a stand, where its light will shine." – **Mark 4:20-21, New Living Translation**

Doesn't it feel wonderful to be counted in the number of those who represent good soil? To be one of those able to hear the Word of God, receive the Word of God, and then be able to apply it. This is where God wants us to be, especially if we are able bodied…people who should know better…who shouldn't just allow the enemy to walk all over us. I know at one point in time, I was counted in the number of folk representing both stony and thorny ground. But thanks be to God for His goodness and mercy…for bearing with me long enough until I got to the place where I could really open up my ears and get an understanding…where I could relate the Word of God to my life and use it to the Glory of God

I realize that none of us are perfect, but just being able to allow the Word of God to minister to our needs gives God Glory…He is pleased with us. But there are many who yet represent stony and thorny ground, and it is up to us "Good Ground" folk to help them get to the place where they can become "Good Ground"…where their ground can be cultivated.

The devil has no new tricks…he just takes the old ones…the very things that he's used to trip us up before…the areas where we are really weak…the places where we have been tried and tested and failed in before, and reuses them on us. You see, the enemy knows our failures. He knows our weaknesses and what intimidates us. He lurks to see how he can get us to fall; or to get us to doubt God. We just have to realize when he is at work in our lives. You see, the enemy does not go after the sinner…he has them already. He comes after you and me…the ones who know who God is…those trying to live a life free of sin…free of worry.

I can remember how the enemy taunted me with all the things I had walked away from when I gave my life back to the Lord…the cares of this world…the riches…the material things…the lustful things… during the time when I represented stony and thorny ground. But I kept coming back to church Sunday after Sunday Bible Study after Bible Study; and then one day the light bulb came on in my head. The pastor would preach a word that made it seem as if he was looking through my window the Friday and Saturday night before. It would happen so often that I began to wonder who I could have talked to at church that would tell that man my business! Then one day I realized that the only reason the light bulb popped on is because the Word of God was beginning to take root and conviction was starting to set in.

Have you ever witnessed a farmer or gardener tilling or plowing dirt? Why do they do it? I'm glad you asked. The purpose behind tilling or plowing is to prepare the ground for planting seed. Take a look at the ground the next time you go outside. On the surface… it is hard…basically unusable for the planting of seed. If a farmer or gardener were to go outside and attempt to plant seed on top of the ground…it is just going to hit the surface and bounce off into another spot. If it manages to find a hole to fall into…it still won't take root because the place under it is still hard (stony). Again, the main purpose of tilling the ground is to soften it up…to dig up old roots from weeds, to turn the ground over or rejuvenate it. Well, that is the purpose of the Word of God…to plow up those things that hinder the seed from taking root in our lives. God wants His Glory…that light to shine in us all, and then He wants us to take that light and allow it to shine in the world…on our jobs… in our homes…in our communities…in the grocery store…on the interstate.,.to our families.

We should be producing a harvest from that light shining in our lives. Producing a thirty, sixty and one-hundred fold harvest of good neighbors…good friends…good co-workers…good family members; just by sharing that light. But don't forget…the devil still knows your weaknesses and he hasn't forgotten about you just because you've allowed that light to come on in your life. You know another thing that a gardener or farmer does? Go ahead, ask me what! Okay, I'm glad you asked. After planting seed and watching that seed take root and grow…he has to maintain its fruit by hoeing. Well, I know you city folks don't know what a hoe is… so I will tell you. A hoe is a gardening tool used to cut away… chop down…mutilate weeds. Its basic use to a gardener is to chop away the weeds growing up around the fruits and vegetables being produced in the garden…to cut down unwanted vines that attempt to choke out the good stuff! Yes…weeds (that old boy-friend or girlfriend that just can't seem to let you go; that old smoking or drinking habit that lingers around…especially when you are having a rough day; that shopping habit that keeps you from paying your tithes; that old lying tongue that just can't seem to tell the truth; that backbiting or badmouth spirit that envelopes you when you want to be pleasant; that man or woman who just gets on your everlasting nerve and makes you want to take your RIGHT foot and….ok watch your mind..LOL! I'm sure you can think of some weeds that have taken root in your life.

Whatever the case, we have to continue to keep our ground "good" by studying God's Word, by fasting and praying, by doing good to others…even when they aren't good to us, by keeping God's commandments, by living the truth. "Let your light so shine before men, that they may see your good works, and Glorify your Father in Heaven" (Matthew 5:16, NKJV). After you get your ground plowed up…share your testimony and help someone else work on their ground.

71

All He Wants is True Thanks

Oh my people listen! For I am your God, listen! Here are my charges against you. I have no complaints of the sacrifices you bring to my altar, for you bring them regularly. But it isn't sacrificial bullocks and goats I really want from you, for all the animals of the field and forest are mine! The cattle on a thousand hills! And all the birds on the mountains! If I were hungry, I would not mention it to you, for all the world is mine and everything in it! No, I don't need your sacrifices of blood and flesh. What I want from you is true thanks; I want your promises fulfilled. I want you to trust me in your times of trouble, so I can rescue you and you can give me glory!

- Psalms 50:7-13 TLB

At my former church, we were taught to not only read the King James Version of the Bible, but to read other translations as well, especially in our times of study. So as I was reading Psalms 50 in the KJV, I also read it in a couple others and was lead to use TLB (The Living Bible) translation. As I began to read this passage in the living translation, I felt as if I was looking up to God…giving Him my undivided, exclusive, complete, entire attention…just as a little girl looks up to her daddy when he is trying to explain something to her; really trying to understand…to comprehend…to grasp what He is saying. Go back and read it again to see if you can feel what I was feeling when I read it.

How did that make you feel? Did it make you want to revisit this past week to see if there was something you had done this week that didn't give glory to God? Was there a moment last week or this past weekend that you experienced something to make you doubt that God is God? Did you say something that didn't give God glory? Did you forget what He has ALREADY done…even if He didn't do anything else? Well, if this word isn't for you…then I will receive it all for myself…because it let's me know that there is something else God wants to do for me and all He wants me to do is be sincere…be genuine…be truthful and honest with my thanks and praise to Him. One Sunday, the Praise and Worship team were going forth and although I can't sing…I was right there with them.

Then mentally, I left the room and there was nobody but me and God! Wow! It was so awesome just being in His presence. Because I served as an announcer, I had to be really focused to know when the praise leader was coming to a close. I forgot that I was announcing that day, when I looked up, he was nodding for me to come up. I went up, but still in the spirit. My face was wet with sweet tears… not tears of pain and sorrow because those tears are salty…but sweet, sweet tears filled with joy…with admonition for the Lord… Abba Father…my father…my King…my Deliver…my Healer…my Provider….my EVERYTHING!! I'm about to lose it all over again… praise be to God!

I took the microphone…still in the spirit and I said "excuse me for the tears," and with the same breath turned it around and shouted why I had the tears. Because God has been good to me…He woke me up another morning and for that I've got to give Him praise. I can't make any excuses for the tears I cry for my God…I can't make any excuses for the joy I have because He has set me free. I could go all day long on that…but that is not where I'm headed. What I'm trying to say…even in recognizing that God has been good to me…there are times when I allow doubt to come into my situation. It is not that I don't believe that God can…but there have been times when my situation looks grim and gloomy, depressing and bleak. So when I read the above passage, it let me know what needs to happen. Either I'm going to trust God concerning my situation… or I'm not. I can't praise and worship and thank Him one day and not the next. I should praise and worship Him every day and in all things…even in the midst of trouble. His word says, "In everything gives Thanks, for this is the Will of God concerning us." God is pleased when He knows that we truly trust Him…that our words, our actions and our thoughts line up with His Word.

He doesn't need anything else from us, but what He said in His Word. He owns everything!! So what else can we give Him? He wants to fulfill our promises. Don't you remember the promises He has made to you? Don't you dare doubt Him…don't you know too much about Him already? Hasn't He already done more than enough? Well, guess what? He wants to do even more…more than you can even imagine. Why? He gets the glory when He rescues you out of your trouble. You know the kind of trouble that nobody can get you out of BUT God; the kind of trouble that requires a miracle; the kind of trouble that nobody else wants to touch. These are the things that give Him glory. Do you have bad credit? Trust God…He wants to erase it because no matter how much money you go and pay to have it erased…it will come back to bite you later. He can erase it and it won't cost you anything but a sincere Thank You Lord! To make that thanks truly sincere is to not go out and mess up what He has just done, because after He's fixed it, He needs to trust you to stay away from all of the high interest credit cards; to drive that car just a little bit longer until you are financially fit to buy a new one, to buy only the things you need…pure necessities and that you only have enough cash for. If it takes credit, you don't need it right now. Wear the clothes you have until He commands the blessing to come your way to get some new ones, and then buy only what you need. I'm sure there are many other areas in our lives where we might be experiencing trouble; you know where yours is, but I dare you to put it before God and watch Him bring deliverance.

There are four things we need to do to prove to God that we want our promises fulfilled. (1) Give Him true thanks; (2) Expect the fulfillment of His promises; (3) Trust God in the midst of our troubles; and (4) Don't forget to give Him the glory. So I challenge you today…and I am taking my own challenge…to put these four nuggets into action in your life every day, so that you can see the manifestation of the Promises of God.

Don't Share It Until It Comes To Pass

And Zacharias said to the angel, "How shall I know this? For I am on old man, and my wife is well advanced in years." And the angel answered and said to him, "I am Gabriel, who stands in the presence of God; and was sent to speak to you and bring you these glad tidings. But behold, you will be mute and not able to speak until the day these things take place, because you did not believe my words which will be fulfilled in their own time."
— Luke 1:18-20, NKJV

Have you ever received a Word from the Lord, whether it was a direct Word to your spirit or from another source that He was going to bless you with something…a nicer car, a bigger home, money, a promotion or a new job, a new wardrobe, the family you've longed for which includes the husband and children, or maybe you have the husband, but God promised the two of you a child. Maybe it was a Word that your dream to be a business owner would come to pass or that He would add a major increase to your current business? Once you got the Word, you weren't just sure how God was going to do it. You weren't sure because you knew that a nicer car meant you needed more money to pay for it, a home larger than the one you have meant you would have to be able to furnish it…let alone pay a bigger house note, and what would be the source of that extra income? Does any of these scenarios sound familiar?

What…me…get a promotion God? I like what I'm doing right now! Do I really want to take on another position or a new job that might require more responsibility? Okay God, I know I haven't come across anyone lately that even mirrors what I desire in a spouse. Kids? I've almost given up on that dream…that's almost next to impossible for me. I don't know that my body will produce a child at this age, and if it did, would I be able to carry it full-term?

I could go on and on with excuses…or should I say doubt that plagues us as a people? In the first chapter of Luke, you will find this situation with Zechariah, an "elderly" priest who served at the temple of Jerusalem. One day as Zechariah stood alone in the temple, the angel Gabriel appeared. He told Zechariah to not be afraid, for his prayer has been heard, and his wife Elizabeth would bear him a son. He then told him to call the child John (Luke 1:13). Now Zechariah found it hard to believe that Elizabeth would join the ranks of Sarah and Hannah, two other infertile women who "miraculously" gave birth in their old age. So what did he do? He showed doubt by asking for a sign. And what did the Lord do? As punishment for his doubt, Gabriel told him that he would remain mute until the child was born. Sure enough, Zechariah could not speak until eight days after his child was born. Elizabeth named the child John instead of after Zechariah, which broke customs set back in those days. After the family protested, Zechariah beckoned for a tablet and wrote that the child's name was to be called John. God restored Zechariah's speech, and He gave praise to the Lord. He then prophesied his son's ministry of being the prophet of the Most High; the one that would go before the Lord to prepare His way. He is known to us as John the Baptist. One thing I learned from reading this story is this; God kept His word...even when Zechariah questioned Him; even after Zechariah doubted that God would perform this miracle. What has God spoken to you that you've cast doubt upon? Just because it hasn't happened yet, does that mean that it won't? Oh ye of little faith.

I said all of that to say this. God is not speaking just to be speaking. He desires that we **believe** not only His written Word, but what He speaks to us through His chosen vessels as well. How can you receive the blessings of God unless you believe? God's word says that faith comes by hearing and hearing by the word of God! You may be one of those who believe everything that the Lord has spoken over your life, but you may have shared it "prematurely" with someone who may have been a dream killer. Remember Moses' story? Remember, the enemy comes to steal, kill, and destroy our dreams and he may do so through people we trust our dreams to. I've heard my pastor say many times that if God showed us everything He is getting ready to do, we would mess it up by getting in the way. This is why He only shows us bits and pieces. There will be times that we will have to be quiet and not share what the Lord has shown us. There will be times that our mouths will have to keep what our hearts have received, because everyone can't handle knowing what God's about to do. If God has spoken something in your spirit or through one of His chosen vessels about what He is getting ready to do for and through you, don't share it until it comes to pass. Only believe!

Are You Getting Godly Council or Mere Opinion?

Blessed is the man that walketh not in the counsel of the ungodly, nor standeth in the way of sinners, nor sitteth in the seat of the scornful. But his delight is in the law of the Lord; and in his law doth he meditate day and night. And he shall be like a tree planted by the rivers of water, that bringeth forth his fruit in his season; his leaf also shall not wither; and whatsoever he doeth shall prosper.
- Psalms 1:1-3 KJV

The book of Psalms is a very powerful light; a light that can speak life into dead situations; a light that will make dark places in our lives become bright again; a light that gives hope where there is none. God's Word is a lamp unto our feet and a light unto our path...but it can only serve its purpose of being a daily guide if we put the Word to use in our lives.

As I was reading this passage, the Holy Spirit directed me back to Job. Job was a perfect and upright man, one who feared God and despised evil. Job offered up a sacrifice daily for his children...He stood in the gap for them, just in case they had sinned against God. He was a great husband, father, employer, and friend. He lived a godly life, and when his world was turned upside down, he still continued to live a godly life. When you look at the first three verses of Psalms, you can pretty much relate them to the character of Job. When God allowed Job to be tested, not once did he turn his back on God...not once did he take the ungodly council of his friends... and neither did he convene with ungodly people.

After Job's friends heard about what he was going through, they didn't come to comfort him, they came to condemn him. Eliphaz spoke up first. Because most of his knowledge is based on his experience, he argued that suffering is a direct result of sin, and sin was the reason behind Job's suffering. He told Job that if he confessed his sins, then his suffering would end. One thing he also stated is that *good* and *innocent* people will not suffer. What if Job had taken the counsel of his friend Eliphaz? Where would he be? I'm glad Job knew who he was. Then we have his friend Bildad. Bildad claimed that the reason Job was suffering was because he wouldn't acknowledge his sin. Then Job's third friend, Zophar decided that he would speak out with power and tell Job that he is lying, and his sufferings are a manifestation of his sins. Don't you find it quite funny that the people who were supposed to know Job the most... really didn't know him at all?

Have you gone through or are you going through something now... where you find those around you trying to give you advice or council concerning your situation; trying to speak into your circumstances when they really don't have a clue about what is going on? The Bible tells us to know them that labour among us; therefore, Job's friends should have known the character of Job. If they really knew him, it would not have been hard for them to accept Job's response... that he was an upright man. All three of Job's friends had made the mistake of assuming that Job had committed some great sin that caused his suffering. Although Job didn't know why he was suffering, he did know that his suffering wasn't due to sin...and therefore didn't lean to the council or advice of his friends.

Have you felt as if you were going through test and trails for no apparent reason? If you are and you know you haven't sinned... then think about Job. God knew what He had in Job...that is why he allowed the test and trials to come upon him. The next time you are in a situation where someone is trying to give you council... make sure it is godly council. Make sure that you know the person from which the information is coming from and you know without a doubt that what they are sharing with you comes from God. Make sure they are godly people. Have they given you solutions in the past that have worked? Do you see the spirit of God working in their lives daily? Have you tried the spirit by the spirit?

Job didn't rely on the opinions of his friends. He didn't curse God as his own wife told him to do...he endured his suffering; and in return, God restored his material blessings and family...and he received even greater blessings than he had before. We will be rewarded if we persist in trusting God. Psalms 1:1-3 explains it better than I ever could and vs. 4-6 lets us know what happens to those who are ungodly. I encourage you today to know where you stand with God...and in knowing where you stand...do all you can to STAND! When things around you are falling apart and you don't have the answer to why...seek God for understanding. And the peace of God, which passeth all understanding, shall keep your hearts and minds through Christ Jesus. (Phil. 4:7) And let the peace of God rule in your hearts, to the which also ye are called in one body, and be ye thankful. (Col. 3:15) Ooooh, if we could just be like Job and wait until our change comes...hold on until God shows up... hang on to God's unchanging hand, then we will reap our rewards just as Job did!

When All You Have Is Bread & Water

And though the Lord give you the bread of adversity, and the water of affliction, yet shall not thy teachers be removed into a corner any more, but thine eyes shall see thy teachers. And thine ears shall hear a word behind thee, saying, This is the way, walk ye in it, when ye turn to the right hand and when ye turn to the left. – Isaiah 30:20-21, KJV

I remember many things about growing up in the projects on the Westside of Chicago. The days in which common tragedies were happening all around us...people shooting people, many doing and selling drugs, people taking their own lives by jumping out of high rise apartment windows, perverts sitting in their car near the corner candy store displaying their private parts to the little girls, people living on the street...sleeping on flattened corrugated boxes, folks getting mugged...purses being snatched...you name it...I saw it. What's really amazing to me is not being able to remember having nothing to eat but bread and water. You would think that if that was all we had in the house...I would remember it...but I don't. My mother recently shared this story with me after I became an adult and I was floored. How can I remember watching her attempt to smoke a cigarette and almost getting choked to death, but not remember that we had nothing to eat but bread and water for weeks...Maybe that is when I learned how to make a syrup sandwich? You think?! When she told me that story, I told her how I remembered the cigarette bit...of course, we had a blast talking about the past. Nevertheless, smoking was not a habit she picked up.

When my mother shared this, it was hard to believe, because I told her that I don't recall NOT EVER having something to eat. And this was true...we never went without eating. What we had to eat may not have been steak and potatoes...but the bread and water was what my mother had to serve us, because she had no other alternative. And when I think about that to this day...I realize that none of us perished by eating our bread and water...as a matter of fact...it helped us to grow into stronger, healthier young men and women.

I realize that Chicago, Illinois is not the only place where things such as those named above happen on a daily basis…it's happening everywhere in the world today. By living in it…witnessing it…I gained a greater appreciation for life, food, and of people. What is adversity and affliction? I want to share with you the synonyms I found on adversity (hardship, difficulty, danger, misfortune, harsh conditions, hard times) and affliction (suffering, burden, problem, pain, trouble, depression despondency, and hopelessness)…sounds like I was sitting right in the midst of it all as a little girl…and didn't have a clue! But while we were eating the bread of adversity and drinking the water of affliction, the Lord protected us…He shielded us and allowed us to come out of it with a testimony. Even the adversity you will face today, tomorrow, or later in the future; whether it comes at you on the job, on the street, or in your home… it will only come to make you better…to increase you…to give you an experience you can share with someone else. It won't kill you.

There is a song that has been blessing me for years, and every time I hear it…I go into tears…because I begin to think about all of the test and trials, tribulations…evil, God has delivered and brought me through. I'm not sure who to give credit to, but it's been sung by numerous gospel artists (Walter Hawkins, Men of Standard, Mary Mary)…just to name a few. The song goes like this:

> *"Tragedies are commonplace, all kinds of diseases, people are slipping away, economy's down…people can't get enough pay, but as for me, all I can say is Thank You Lord for all you've done for me. Folks without homes, people are in the streets. And the drug habit some say, they just can't beat. Muggers and robbers, no place seems to be safe; But you've been my protection every step of the way, and I want to say, Thank You Lord for all you've done for me."*

As this song ministers to the children of God, it should be a driving force of encouragement to let you know that God can and will protect you…but you have to trust Him. The enemy will do his best to bring destruction…despair…to inundate us with the cares of this world…to flood our hearts and our minds with worry…to magnify issues in our lives that are small in the eyes of God. He will flood us with sorrow, greed, lust, enmity, poverty, selfishness, pride, hatred, hurt and pain. But Isaiah 59:19b reads, "When the enemy comes in like a flood, the Spirit of the Lord shall lift up a standard against him." God will come to our defense just like a rushing stream. And just when the enemy thinks he's got you... God snatches you from the clutches of the enemy and brings you to a place of peace...of hope...of abundant life. When you are served the bread of adversity and water of affliction...get out the knife, the fork and your napkin...then eat, drink and be merry!!

Strategy for Prosperity

This book of the law shall not depart out of thy mouth; but thou shalt meditate therein day and night, that thou mayest observe to do according to all that is written therein: for then thou shalt make thy way prosperous, and then thou shalt have good success. Have not I commanded thee? Be strong and of a good courage; be not afraid, neither be thou dismayed: for the Lord thy God is with thee whithersoever thou goest. – Joshua 1:9

If I were to ask you the question, how do you measure success... what would your answer be? Would you allow your success to rest in the hands of another being or would you want to take complete control and responsibility for your own success? I've learned over time that measuring your success by others' standards is not success...neither is measuring your success by others' failures.

I was formerly employed with a company that charted the growth of their employees through a process called succession planning. The supervisors and managers met on a regular basis to identify employees who had the potential to be future leaders within the department. Their goal was to identify the individual's skills and then guide this person's career in the direction they thought this person would be most successful. Now, keep in mind...the employee's input is not considered in this process because they are not given an opportunity to voice their opinion or share their short and long term goals for themselves. Someone else is responsible for making those decisions for them.

In my case, it was not my desire to do the job they had identified for me. I was told that I would receive a pay increase for working in this particular position whenever the other individual was out of the office. At the time, I was okay with that, but quickly realized that this was a tactic to keep me in the department and keep me from progressing to where "I" wanted to go. This meant that I was putting my success in the hands of others...and I was not going for that. I decided that I had a right to chart my own career path and make the decisions on where I wanted to work and what I wanted to be. Didn't God give me that right? And because of that, I took the control of my future out of their hands.

Are you one of those who think prosperity is based on power, influence, or who you know? There are many who feel this way. God was teaching Joshua against these types of methods. He gave Joshua the strategy for prosperity: (1) be strong and brave because the task ahead would not be easy, (2) Obey God's Law, and (3) constantly read and study God's Word. Although this is not the world's standards, we can be successful in the eyes of God if we follow these three commands. If we work diligently to put these commands into action in our lives, God promises that He will be with us wherever we go. Not only that, but when we put God's plan into action in our lives, He ultimately charts our paths and puts us in places we would have never gotten on our own; jobs we aren't qualified for. The plan of man is one thing, but they can't compare to God's plans and favor on our lives.

Invite The Holy Spirit into Your Prayer Closet

But ye, beloved, building up yourselves on your most holy faith, praying in the Holy Ghost. Keep yourselves in the love of God, looking for the mercy of our Lord Jesus Christ unto eternal life.
                                                        - Jude 20-21, KJV

Do you have days when you fall on your knees to pray...you just can't find the words to say? Maybe it's not that you can't find the words...but maybe you don't want to be monotonous in your prayer to the Lord. You want to make sure that you are not saying the same old thing every time you bend your knees. I have found myself in that place on many occasions. The first thing I do when I get down to pray is praise and adore God for who He is...He is good, He is merciful...He is kind...He is magnificent and precious to me because He loved me enough to send His Son to die for me. Then I offer up thanks for just waking me up another morning... letting me see another day...for protecting me through dangers seen and unseen...shielding me from accidents...keeping my family safe and healthy...giving me a good job...a roof over my head...food on the table and clothes on our backs. Then I get to the place where I'm searching for words...I don't know what to pray for next...I'm not sensing a particular person or thing in my spirit that I need to pray for or about...yet I know that I should be interceding for someone else because I know that God knows I'm grateful for all of the things He has given me and done for me because I make it a point to tell Him every day.

So this is where I shut up. I pause for a moment of silence. I remain still and allow the Holy Spirit to come in and take over. I know that even my little finite mind doesn't compare to the mind of Christ, and if I allow the Spirit to take over my prayer...He's going to make sure that those things I really need to pray about will get prayed for. It is here, in my quietness...in my state of complete stillness... that the Holy Spirit begins to reveal to me who and what I need to pray for. He begins dropping people into my Spirit; situations that I haven't considered; people close to me who may be hiding within their hurt and don't have the courage to ask someone else to pray for them. But if I get up too quickly, once I've prayed for myself, then I might miss the opportunity to intercede on someone else's behalf. I may miss what the Holy Spirit is trying to reveal to me; all because I got up too quickly, all because I was in a rush to get back to the mundane things of life, all because I didn't have time to listen to God. Communication is a two way process...sending and receiving. If only one person is talking, then there is no communication... you're just talking. In prayer, you send up your requests and God sends down His response. God doesn't want you to be the only one talking. He has something to say too. But all too often we're focused on what God can do for us, not what we can do for God; and many times, all He wants is for someone to stand in the gap for others... and that won't cost us anything but time.

There are people around you today that stand in the need of something from God. It could be emotional healing, it could be physical healing. it could be that a loved one needs protection or to be saved, it could be a financial breakthrough; in whatever case, when you go into your prayer closet...after there are no more words to say, just sit quiet for a moment. You may be surprised what things God reveals to you in that quiet time. Before you know it, your five minute prayer has turned into 15 minutes, then 30 or 45...or maybe you've completely lost track of time. Once we learn to allow the Holy Spirit to have His way in our prayer time, you will have prayed for people that you had no clue to pray for, and God will be glorified. Don't get me wrong, it's not about the length of your prayer. God is not sitting up in heaven with a time clock recording the number of minutes that we spend in prayer. God is looking at our hearts and its sincerity.

I believe God wants to say something to you in your prayer time today. Do you have time to listen? If you do, then don't hesitate to invite the Holy Spirit into your prayer closet.

Tough Love Is Better Than No Love

And ye have forgotten the exhortation which speaketh unto you as unto children, My son, despise not thou the chastening of the Lord, nor faint when thou art rebuked of Him: For whom the Lord loveth He chasteneth, and scourgeth every son whom He receiveth. Hebrews 12:5-6

I've heard it said that when a parent doesn't discipline their child then it means they don't love them. This is true...and the Bible tells us so. If you pay attention when you go out in public, you will be able to witness the difference between a child who receives chastisement and one that does not. The difference is, the child who has been administered correction is the child that demonstrates respect, whereas the child without discipline is the child who demonstrates disrespect...they have no regard for what is going on and no regard for the person administering the discipline. A child with no discipline in his or her life is just like a ship without a sail...being tossed to and fro while on the sea; he or she is a child with no restraint...nothing to reel him or her in when they get out of line. They are basically on a path to destruction.

Discipline is used to guide wrong behavior...to steer one's action on the right path. If someone is allowed to continue in the wrong, then they will never be fully developed. Chastisement is like vision, and where there is none, the people will perish. In most cases we don't want to be chastised. Think about a scenario in your life where you were chastised, disciplined, reprimanded, or punished; whether as a child or an adult. How did you respond to it? Did you resent it? Did it anger you? Did you despise it? Most of us react in all of those examples. I was chastised on a previous job for coming in late just about every day. It may have been only five minutes...but I was late...sometimes it was only one or two minutes, but I was late. My job required me to have the telephone lines on and the vault opened by 8:00 a.m. If someone called the office and I wasn't on my post, they could easily report to my supervisor that our office isn't opening up on time. I wasn't the only person working in that office or the only person required to be in the office by 8:00 a.m. There were three other people, plus the manager who were due in at the same time. Guess what? They all came in much later than I did, but I was the one being monitored. I was the one being reported as if it didn't matter what time the others came in. Did I resent this happening? Of course I did...as any normal person would resent being corrected. The sad part about it all is...I was only being late because they were being late and it seemed to be okay with the manager. It didn't matter that I knew better...I wanted to be like everyone else instead of being the one who was "different," or should I say, in the right. What was wrong with that...hmmm?

One particular day the manager came in before 8:00. Right then and there I knew it was a setup. How did I know? That day I was late, but the others came in on-time. I didn't expect the manager to say anything, but it was all a setup. I was called into the office and reprimanded for my tardiness. Boy was I fuming on the inside... man was I hot!! I was angry for allowing myself to be setup, and I was also resentful of the supervisor's chastisement. But it was God's way of administering to me "Tough Love." The Bible tells us in verse 11 (NLT) *"No discipline is enjoyable while it is happening... it is painful! But afterward, there will be a quiet harvest of right living for those who are trained in this way."*

My moment of correction turned my tardiness around. I began to get to work thirty minutes earlier than required and because of that, I was able to change my work hours and leave thirty minutes earlier each day. Of course, this angered my co-workers because there was motive behind getting me caught. In the end, it backfired, but it also got me back on the right track. We have to remember that if no one else does the right thing, we, as children of God are required to do the right thing! If you have children, don't be afraid to use tough love with them. My oldest daughter used to get angry at me for not allowing her to go and hang out at the movie theater with her buddies. I was afraid for her and what could happen if I took her and just dropped her off at the movie theater with no supervision. Not only that, but how would God react to me as a mother by taking my child and dumping her on a curb to hang out? Well guess what...more parents are doing this everyday without realizing the impact. Oh, I'm sure she wore me out in her mind, under her breath, and behind my back, but I had to show some tough love. When chastisement comes, don't resent it...embrace it because God is showing you how much He loves you. Always remember, God wants nothing but the best for us... and if He has to use chastisement to cause us to get back in line, guess what...He will use it. His love is better than no love...those He chastens, He loves.

Let Your Testimony Be Your Witness

But you shall receive power when the Holy Spirit has come upon you; and you shall be witnesses to Me in Jerusalem, and in all Judea and Samaria, and to the end of the earth."

- Acts 1:8 NKJV

Do you find yourself struggling with what to say and how to say it when you've been faced with an opportunity to minister? How do you know if what you have said was effective? I've learned that people are looking for something to believe in; they want realness and truth; someone to relate their situation to and someone who shares in their struggle. The very people, who share the struggle you can bear witness to, will be the people you will find yourself ministering to. If God has blessed you to overcome your area of struggle, then He will give you the words that will minister to the soul of another who is looking for hope. Understand that when it is time for you to minister...God will provide the platform, so you must be ready and sensitive to the move of God.

The scripture above tells us that "when" we have received the Holy Ghost..."when"...we shall be endued with power. That power comes to help us walk right...to talk right...to live right...and to help the next person in their struggle. Next it says that we shall be witnesses unto God. How will we become witnesses unto God? We become witnesses when we simply share with others what the Lord has done for us. While at a tent revival my pastor was holding some years ago, we had some good old testimonial service. I was challenged to share in my area of struggle, and I was not afraid because I was determined to be delivered in that area, which was fornication. You see, fornication is running rampant in our churches. Satan has deceived the believer into thinking that it is okay to lie down as long as you get back up. Yes, once you ask for forgiveness...God can and will forgive you; BUT, there are consequences for the sin... God is holding us accountable for everything we do outside of His commandments. God's Word doesn't lie.

Ephesians 6:12 says, "For we wrestle not against flesh and blood, but against principalities, against powers, against the rulers of the darkness of this world, against spiritual wickedness in high places." Every time a person sins, they get entangled with the prince of darkness, the ruler of this world. Sometimes it is hard to break away from the devil once you get entangled with him. I am a witness to this and you may be also. So here is where you can be of help to the kingdom. As I was sharing earlier about the tent revival, I gave the devil notice that he would no longer keep me bound. Because I wasn't afraid to share where I had been, other young ladies wrote to me, or called me, or even stopped me to say how they too had been deceived by the enemy in that area. Sharing your testimony of deliverance is a witness to God...as He said you would be.

It is only God who can deliver us from the clutches of the enemy and when He does...He wants us to go and share it with someone else who may need to know that He is REAL...and that He is yet working miracles. Remember the man with the unclean spirit in the 5th chapter of Mark? After Jesus called the spirit out of the man and sent it into the swine, he told the man to go home to his friends, and tell them of the great things the Lord had done. The man did so and others marveled...they were amazed...they believed. Even as we continue to read about the miracles Jesus performed...you see where many people "heard" about what He had done for others and because they needed deliverance too, they searched Him out, they tried to touch Him when He walked by, they called out to Him. And so it is today; people are still looking for someone and something to believe in. We have to give them real life experiences... testimonies of deliverance...of blessings…of His saving grace.

So I challenge you today to let your testimony be your witness of the goodness and mercies of God. I can say today, that if it had not been for God's grace and mercy towards me, I would be sitting behind a jail cell...or 6 feet under in my grave. Don't hesitate to share your testimony with someone who needs it!

Bible References

Online Bible: Bible Resoures.org

> *King James Bible Version*
> *The Message Bible Version*
> *New American Standard Bible Version*
> *Amplified Bible Version*
> *The New King James Version*